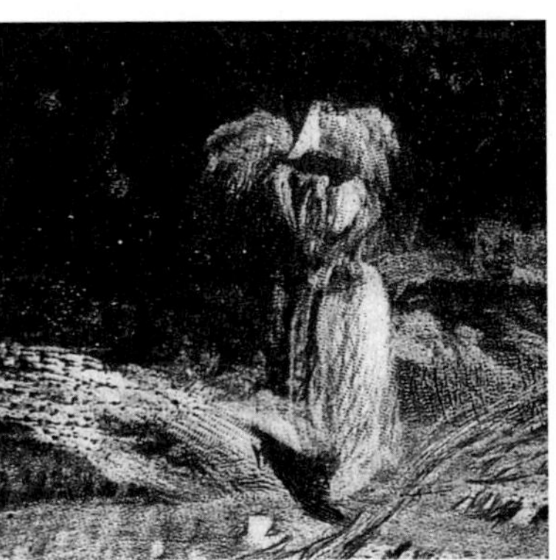

English Landscape.

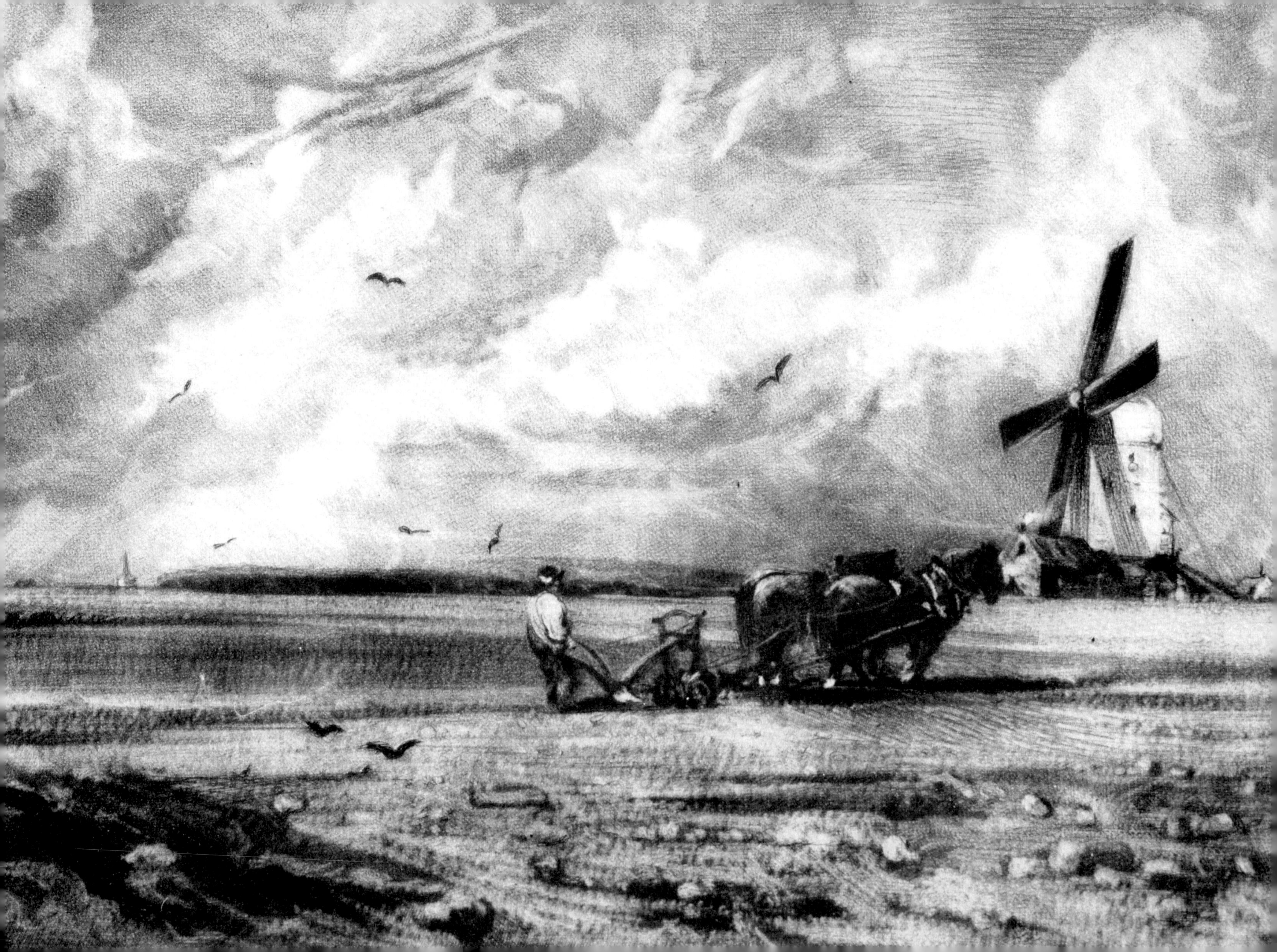

VARIOUS SUBJECTS OF

LANDSCAPE,

CHARACTERISTIC OF ENGLISH SCENERY,

FROM PICTURES PAINTED BY

JOHN CONSTABLE, R. A.

ENGRAVED BY

DAVID LUCAS.

London:

PUBLISHED BY MR. CONSTABLE, 35, CHARLOTTE STREET, FITZROY SQUARE.

SOLD BY COLNAGHI, DOMINIC COLNAGHI, AND CO. PALL MALL EAST.

1830.

John Constable R. A.

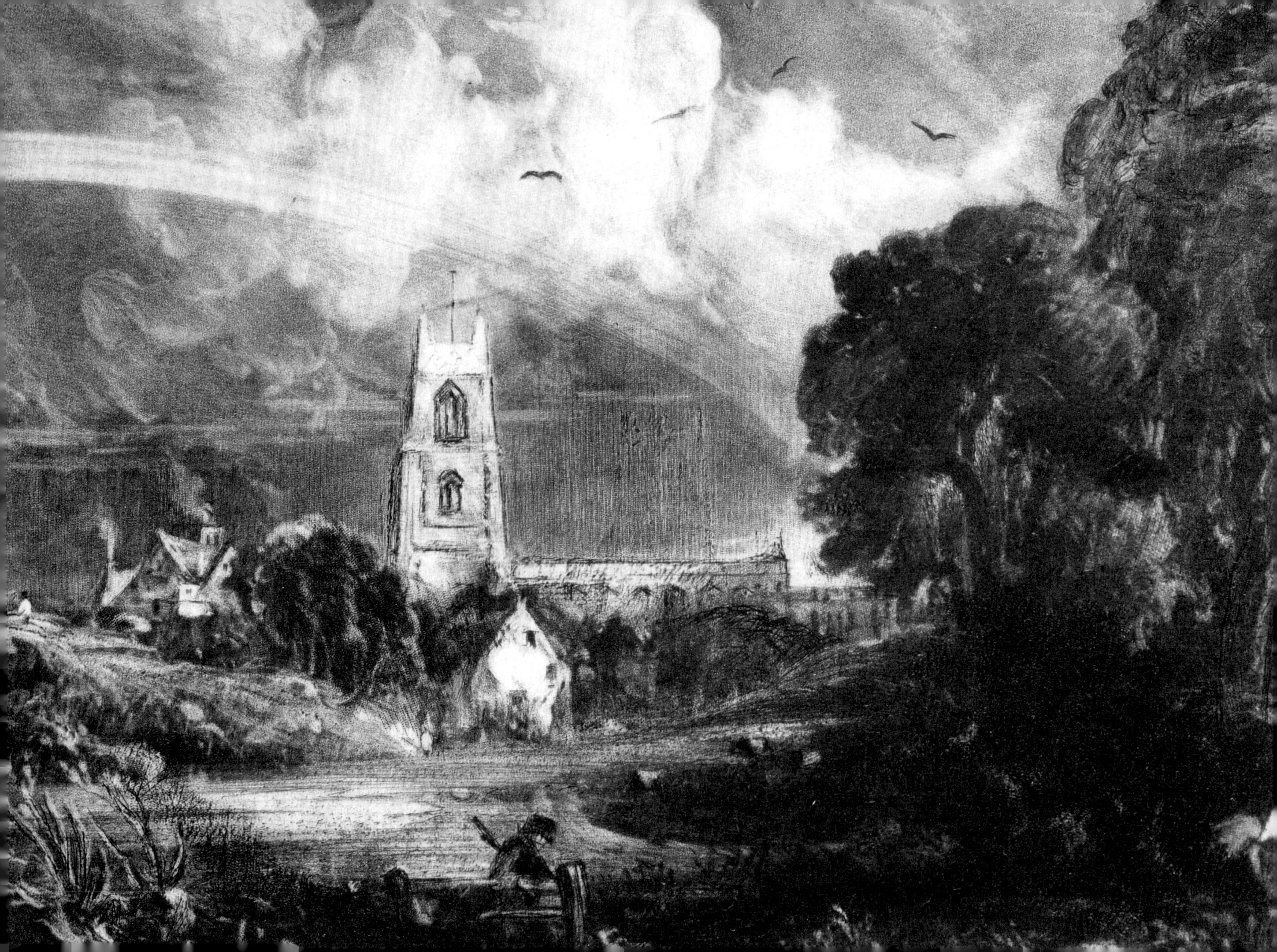

TABLE OF CONTENTS

INTRODUCTION

Rura mihi, et rigui placeant in vallibus amnes,
Flumina amem, sylvasque, inglorius. – Virgil.*

THE AUTHOR RESTS IN THE BELIEF that the present collection of prints of rural landscape may not be found wholly unworthy of attention. It originated in no mercenary views, but merely as a pleasing professional occupation, and was continued with a hope of imparting pleasure and instruction to others. He had imagined to himself certain objects in art, and has always pursued them. Much of the landscape, forming the subject of these plates, going far to embody his ideas (owing perhaps to the rich and feeling manner in which they are engraved) he has been tempted to publish them, and offers them as the result of his own experience, founded as he conceives it to be in a just observation of natural scenery in its various aspects. From the almost universal esteem in which the arts are now held, the author is encouraged to hope that this work may not be found unacceptable, since perhaps no branch of the art offers a more inviting field of study than landscape.

> Soul-soothing Art! whom morning, noon-tide, even,
> Do serve with all their fitful pageantry.†

The immediate aim of the author in this publication is to increase the interest for, and promote the study of, the rural scenery of England, with all its endearing associations, its amenities, and even its most simple localities; abounding as it does in grandeur, and every description of pastoral beauty: England, with her climate of more than vernal freshness, and in whose summer skies, and rich autumnal clouds, 'with thousand liveries dight,'§ the student of Nature may daily watch her endless varieties of effect, for by him it is, that these changes are particularly observed: "Multa vident Pictores in imminentia et in umbris quae nos non videmus." – Cicero.‡

It is therefore perhaps in its professional character that this work may be most considered, so far as it respects the ART; its aim being to direct attention to the source of one of its most efficient principles, the 'CHIAR'OSCURO OF NATURE,' to mark the influence of light and shadow upon landscape, not only in its general effect on the 'whole,' and as a means of rendering a proper emphasis on the 'parts,' in painting, but also to show its use and power as a medium of expression, so as to note 'the day, the hour, the sunshine, and the shade.' In some of these subjects of landscape an attempt has been made to arrest the

* *Georgics* II, lines 485–6. 'Let my delight be the country, and the running streams amid the dells – may I love the waters and the woods, though I be unknown to fame' (trans H. Rushton Fairclough). † William Wordsworth, 'Upon the Sight of a Beautiful Picture Painted by Sir G. H. Beaumont, Bt.' (1811), lines 9-10. Constable has substituted 'fitful' for 'changeful'. § Approximate quotation from John Milton's *L'Allegro*. ‡ Approximate quotation from Cicero's *Academica*, II, 7: 'How many things painters see in shadows and in the foreground which we do not see! (trans. H. Rackham).

more abrupt and transient appearances of the CHIAR'OSCURO IN NATURE; to show its effect in the most striking manner, to give 'to one brief moment caught from fleeting time,'* a lasting and sober existence, and to render permanent many of those splendid but evanescent exhibitions, which are ever occurring in the changes of external Nature.

In the selection of these subjects, a partiality has perhaps been given to those of a particular neighbourhood: some of them, however, may be more generally interesting, as the scenes of many of the marked historical events of our middle ages. The most of these subjects, chiefly consisting of home scenery, are from the pictures exhibited by the author at the Royal Academy during the last few years; they are taken from real places, and are meant particularly to characterize the scenery of England; the effects of light and shadow being transcripts only of such as occurred at the time of being taken.

In art as in literature, however, there are two modes by which men endeavour to attain the same end, and seek distinction. In the one, the artist, intent only on the study of departed excellence, or on what others have accomplished, becomes an imitator of their works, as he selects and combines their various beauties; in the other he seeks perfection at its PRIMITIVE SOURCE, NATURE. The one, forms a style upon the study of pictures, or the art alone; and produces, either 'imitative', 'scholastic', or that which has been termed the 'Eclectic Art. The other, by study equally legitimately founded in art, but further pursued in such a far more expansive field, soon finds for himself innumerable sources of study, hitherto unexplored, fertile in beauty, and by attempting to display them for the first time, forms a style which is original; thus adding to the art, qualities of Nature unknown to it before. The results of the one mode, as they merely repeat what has been done by others, and by having the appearance of that with which the eye is already familiar, can be easily comprehended, soon estimated, and are at once received. Thus the rise of an artist in a sphere of his own must almost certainly be delayed; it is to time generally that the justness of his claims to a lasting reputation will be left; so few appreciate any deviation from a beaten track, can trace the indications of talent in immaturity, or are qualified to judge of productions bearing an original cast of mind, of genuine study, and of consequent novelty of style in their mode of execution.

J. C.

35, Charlotte Street, Fitzroy Square, May, 1833.

† William Wordsworth, op. cit., line 13.

FRONTISPIECE: EAST BERGHOLT, SUFFOLK

House of the late Golding Constable, Esq.,
and birthplace of the artist

The Latin tag, from 'Laus sapientiæ divinæ' by Alexander Neckham (1157-1217), can be translated as 'This place knew the beginnings of our age/ Happy years and days of joy./ This place imbued our innocent boyhood years/With the arts and was the origin of our fame.'

FRONTISPIECE.

To Mr. Constable's English Landscape.

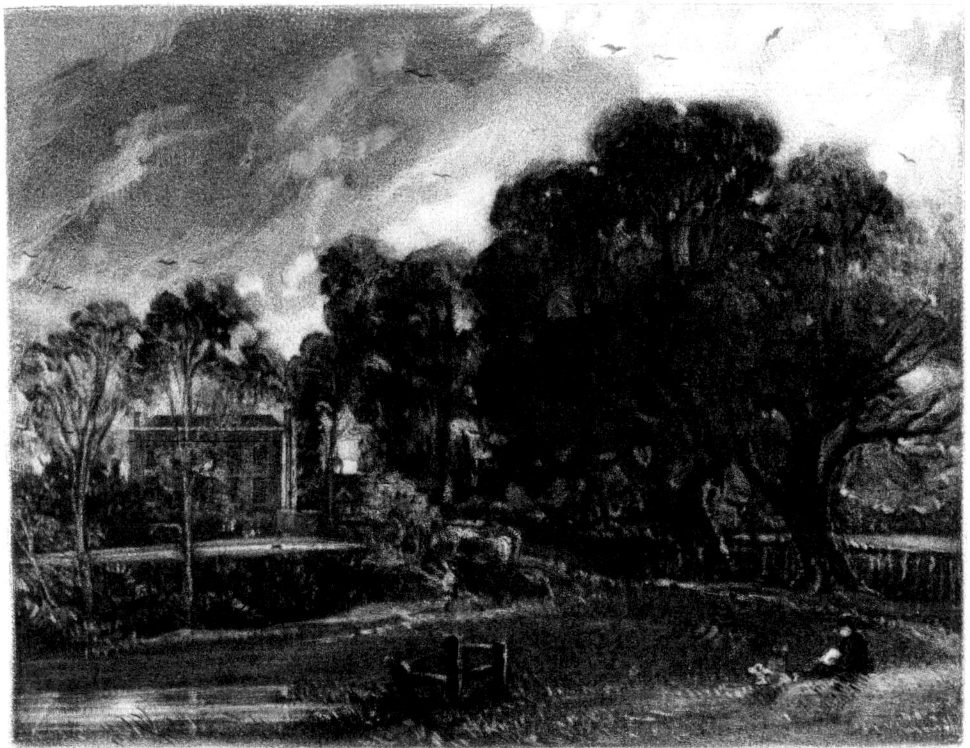

Painted by John Constable, R.A. — Engraved by David Lucas.

EAST BERGHOLT, SUFFOLK.

"Hic locus ætatis nostræ primordia novit
Annos felices lætitiaque dies:
Hic locus ingenuis pueriles imbuit annos
Artibus, et nostræ laudis origo fuit."

London Published by Mr. Constable 35 Charlotte St. Fitzroy Square 1831

EAST BERGHOLT, SUFFOLK
The house and grounds of the late Golding Constable, Esq.

*Respiciens rura, laremque suam.**

With frequent foot
Pleased have I , in my cheerful morn of life,
When nursed by careless Solitude I lived
And sung of Nature with unceasing joy,
Pleased have I wandered o'er your fair domain.†

As this work was begun and pursued by the author solely with a view of his own feelings, as well as his own notions of art, he may be pardoned for introducing a spot to which he must naturally feel so much attached; and though to others it may be void of interest or any associations, to him it is fraught with every endearing recollection.

In this plate the endeavour has been to give, by richness of light and shadow, an interest to a subject otherwise by no means attractive. The broad still lights of a summer evening, with the solemn and far-extended shadows cast around by the intervening objects, small portions of them only and of the landscape gilded by the setting sun, cannot fail to give an interest to the most simple or barren subject, and even to mark it with pathos and effect.

East Bergholt, or as its Saxon derivation implies, 'Wooded Hill,' is thus mentioned in *The Beauties of England and Wales*: – 'South of the church is "Old Hall," the Manor House, the seat of Peter Godfrey, Esq., which, with the residences of the rector, the Reverend Dr. Rhudde, Mrs. Roberts, and Golding Constable, Esq., give this place an appearance far superior to that of most villages.'§ It is pleasantly situated in the most cultivated part of Suffolk, on a spot which overlooks the fertile valley of the Stour, which river divides that county on the south from Essex. The beauty of the surrounding scenery, the gentle declivities, the luxuriant meadow flats sprinkled with flocks and herds, and well cultivated uplands, the woods and rivers, the numerous scattered villages and churches, with farms and picturesque cottages, all impart to this particular spot an amenity and elegance hardly anywhere else to be found; and which has always caused it to be admired by all persons of taste, who have been lovers of painting, and who can feel a pleasure in its pursuit when united with the contemplation of nature.‡

* Shortened quotation from Ovid, *Tristia* III, line 62, 'Gazing back [...] upon their farms and their homes.' Constable omitted the word 'frustra' – 'in vain'. † James Thomson, *The Four Seasons: Winter*, lines 6–10. The last four words have been altered: they should read 'through your rough domain'. § Frederic Shoberl, *The Beauties of England and Wales*, vol. XIV, 1813, p. 225 ‡ Note by Constable: The late Dr. John Fisher, Bishop of Exeter, and afterwards Bishop of Salisbury, and also the late Sir George Beaumont, Baronet, both well known as admirers and patrons of Painting, often passed their summers at Dedham, the adjoining village to Bergholt; to the latter of whom the Author was happily introduced through the anxious and parental attention of his Mother; and for his truly valuable acquaintance with Dr. Fisher, he was indebted to the kindness of his early friends, the Hurlocks – of which circumstance he has a lively and grateful remembrance. These events entirely influenced his future life, and were the foundation of a sincere and uninterrupted friendship, which terminated but with the lives of these estimable men.

Perhaps the Author with an over-weening affection for these scenes may estimate them too highly, and may have dwelt too exclusively upon them; but interwoven as they are with his thoughts, it would have been difficult to have avoided doing so; besides, every recollection associated with the Vale of Dedham must always be dear to him, and he delights to retrace those scenes, 'where once his careless childhood strayed,'† among which the happy years of the morning of his life were passed, and where by a fortunate chance of events he early met those, by whose valuable and encouraging friendship he was invited to pursue his first youthful wish, and to realize his cherished hopes, and that ultimately led to fix him in that pursuit to which he felt his mind directed: and where is the student of landscape, who in the ardour of youth, would not willingly forgo the vainer pleasures of society, and seek his reward in the delights resulting from the love and study of nature, and in his successful attempts to imitate her in the features of the scenery with which he is surrounded; so that in whatever spot he may be placed, he shall be impressed with the beauty and majesty of nature under all her appearances, and, thus, be led to adore the hand that has, with such lavish beneficence, scattered the principles of enjoyment and happiness throughout every department of the Creation. It was in scenes such as these, and he trusts with such a feeling, that the author's ideas of landscape were formed; and he dwells on the retrospect of those happy days and years 'of sweet retired solitude,' passed in the calm of an undisturbed congenial study, with a fondness and delight which must ever be to him a source of happiness and contentment.

Nature! enchanting Nature! in whose form
And lineaments divine I trace a hand
That errs not, and find raptures still renew'd,
Is free to all men – universal prize.†

* Adapted from Thomas Gray, 'Ode on a distant prospect of Eton College' (1742), line 13.

† William Cowper, *The Task*, Book III, lines 721–724. The exclamation marks are not in the original.

I: SPRING

East Bergholt Common

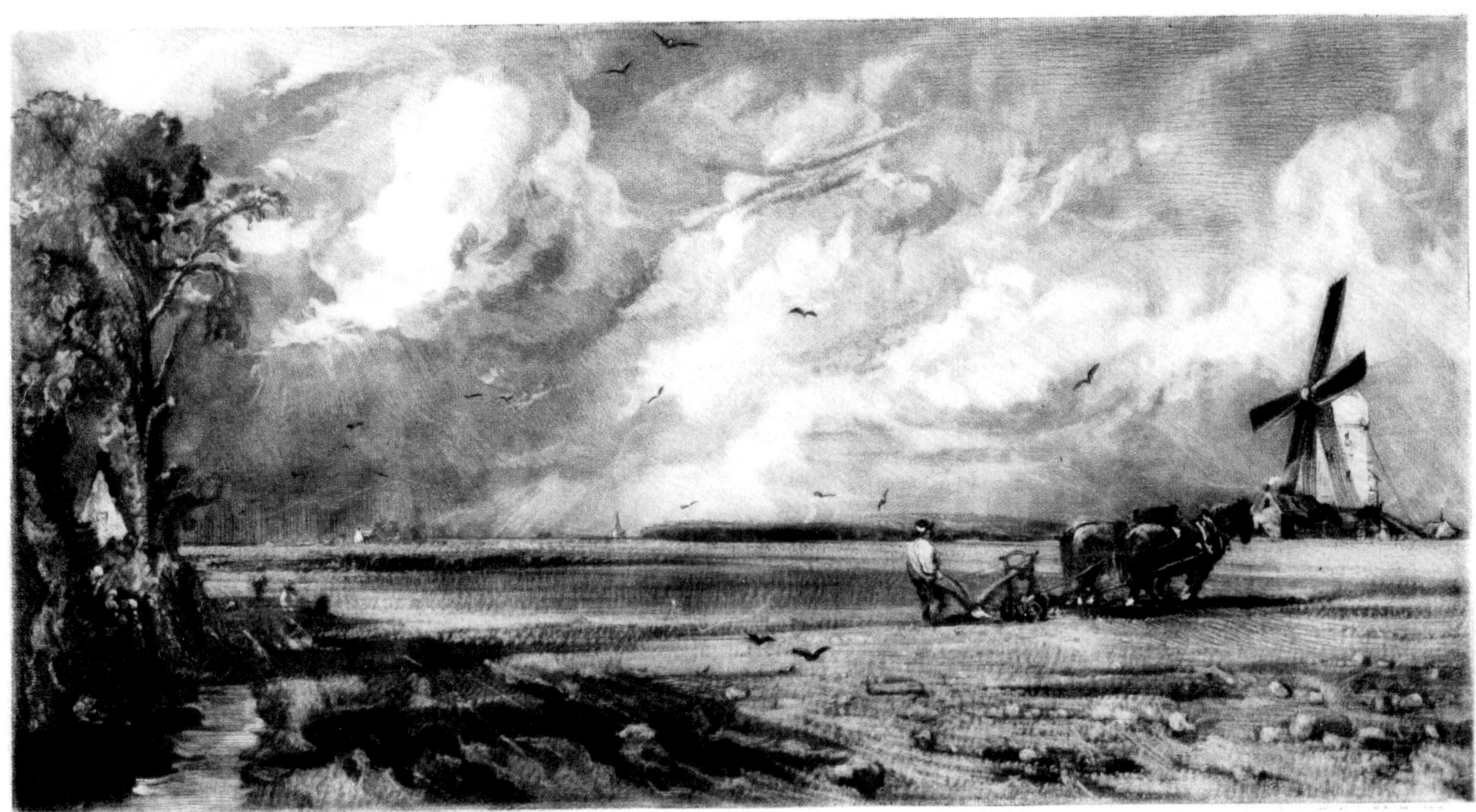

SPRING

Hence the breath
Of life informing each organic frame;
Hence the green earth, and wild resounding waves;
Hence light and shade alternate, warmth and cold,
And bright and dewy clouds, and vernal show'rs,
And all the fair variety of things.*

This plate may perhaps give some idea of one of those bright and animated days of the early year, when all nature bears so exhilarating an aspect; when at noon large garish clouds, surcharged with hail or sleet, sweep with their broad cool shadows the fields, woods, and hills; and by the contrast of their depths and bloom enhance the value of the vivid greens and yellows, so peculiar to this season; heightening also their brightness, and by their motion causing that playful change, always so much desired by the painter.

The natural history – if the expression may be used – of the skies above alluded to, which are so particularly marked in the hail squalls at this time of the year, is this: – the clouds accumulate in very large and dense masses, and from their loftiness seem to move but slowly: immediately upon these large clouds appear numerous opaque patches, which, however, are only small clouds passing rapidly before them, and consisting of isolated pieces, detached probably from the larger cloud. These floating much nearer the earth, may perhaps fall in with a stronger current of wind, which as well as their comparative lightness, causes them to move with greater rapidity; hence they are called by wind-millers and sailors 'messengers,' being always the forerunners of bad weather. They float about midway in what may be termed the lanes of the clouds; and from being so situated, are almost uniformly in shadow, receiving only a reflected light from the clear blue sky immediately above, and which descends perpendicularly upon them into these lanes. In passing over the bright parts of the large clouds, they appear as 'darks'; but in passing the shadowed parts they assume a gray, a pale, or lurid hue.

Fair-handed Spring unbosoms every grace.†

The autumn only is called the painter's season, from the great richness of the colours of the dead and decaying foliage, and the peculiar

* Mark Akenside, *The Pleasures of Imagination. A poem.* (1744), lines 73–78. The phrase 'And bright and dewy clouds' has been substituted for 'And clear autumnal skies'.

† James Thomson, *The Four Seasons: Spring,* (1730), line 489.

tone and beauty of the skies; but the spring has perhaps more than an equal claim to his notice and admiration, and from causes not wholly dissimilar – the great variety of tints and colours of the living foliage, besides having the flowers and blossoms. The beautiful and tender hues of the young leaves and buds are rendered more lovely by being contrasted, as they now are, with the sober russet browns of the trees and hedges from which they shoot, and which still shew the drear remains of the season that is past. The tender beauties which wait upon this flowery season are but too often premature; the early blights and 'killing frosts'* which usually attend it have caused the fickleness of spring to be proverbial, even with the poets, who feelingly allude to it – 'Abortive as the first-born bloom of spring':† – their genius, however, has made it a source of the most beautiful and touching imagery.

Hoary-headed frosts
Fall in the fresh lap of the crimson rose;
And on old Hyems' chin and icy crown
An od'rous chaplet of sweet summer buds
Is as in mockery set.§

The ploughman 'leaning o'er the shining share,'‡ the sower 'stalking with measured step the neighbouring fields,'** are conspicuous objects in the vernal landscape; and last, though not least in interest, the birds, 'by the great Father of the Spring inspired,'†† who with their songs again cheer the labourer at his work, and complete the joyous animation of the new season.

* Untraced. † John Milton, *Samson Agonistes*, (1671), Book III, line 1576. § William Shakespeare, *A Midsummer Night's Dream*, (1595 or 1596) Act II, Scene I, lines 110-114. ‡ James Thomson, *The Four Seasons: Spring*, (1730), lines 40-41. The original reads 'incumbent o'er the shining share/The master leans'.

** James Thomson, *The Four Seasons: Spring*, (1730), lines 44-45. The original reads 'through the neighbouring fields the sower stalks/With measur'd step'. †† James Thomson, *The Four Seasons: Spring*, (1730), line 640.

2: AUTUMNAL SUN SET

Peasants returning homeward

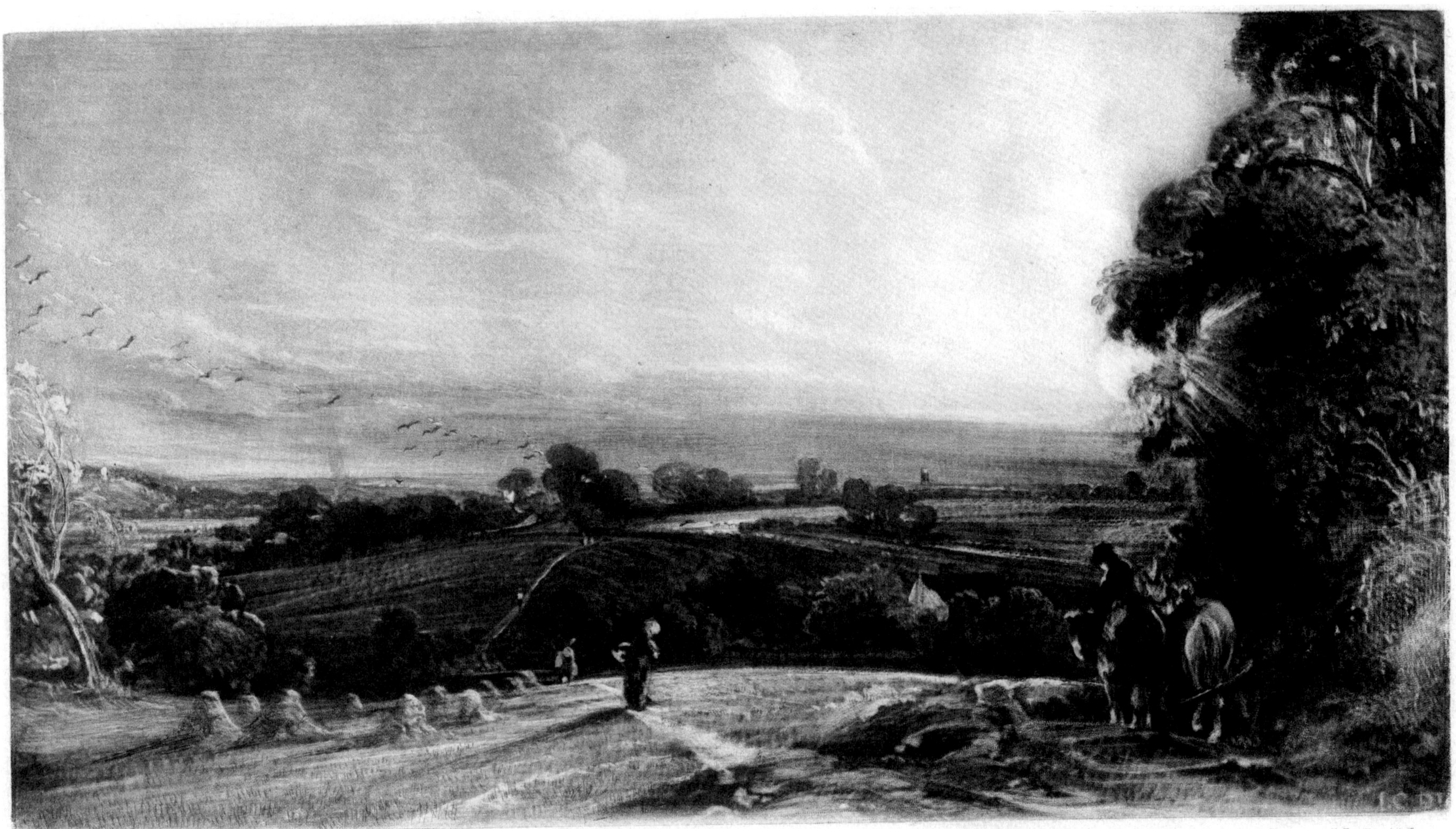

3: NOON

West End Fields, Hampstead

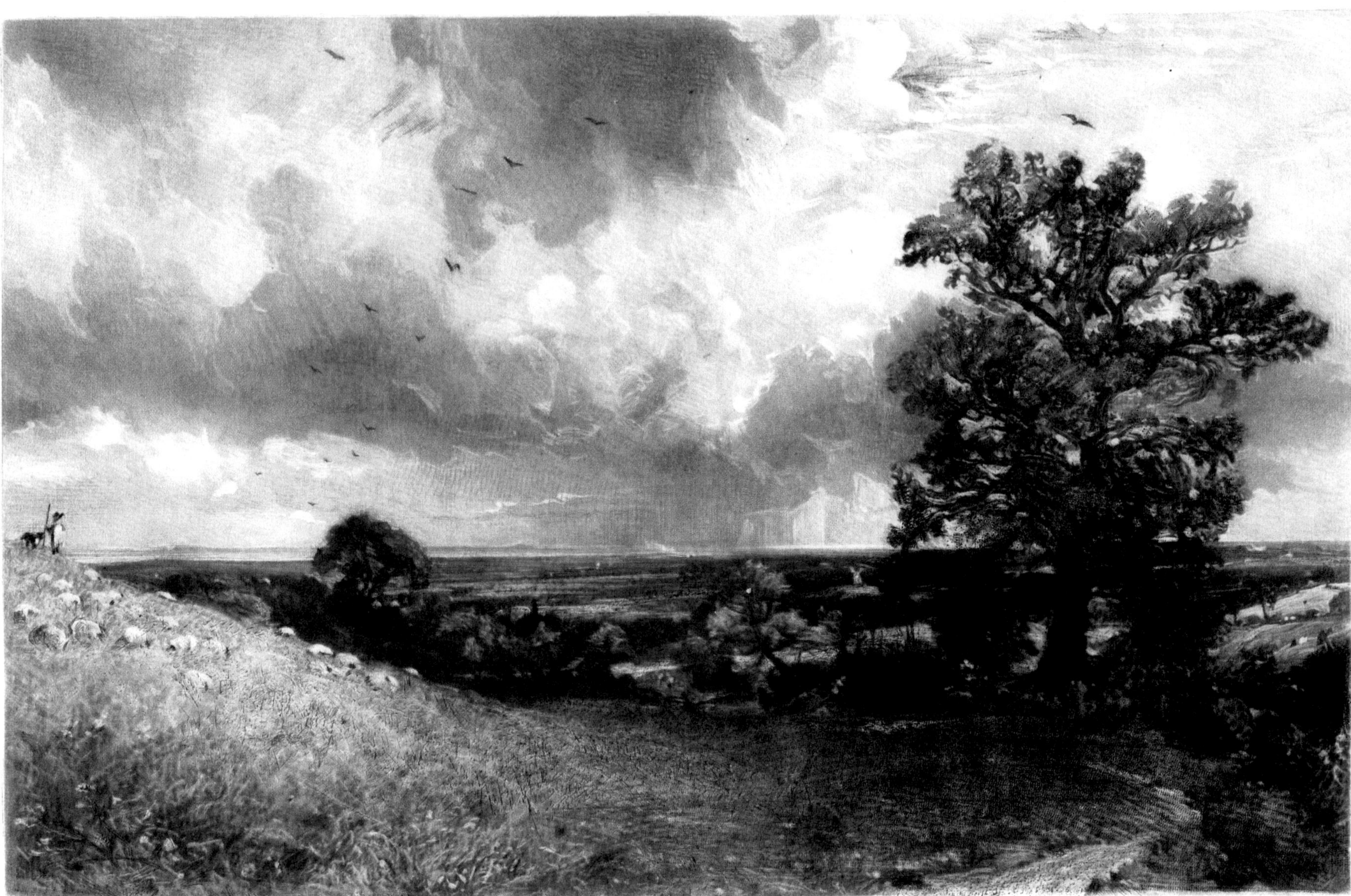

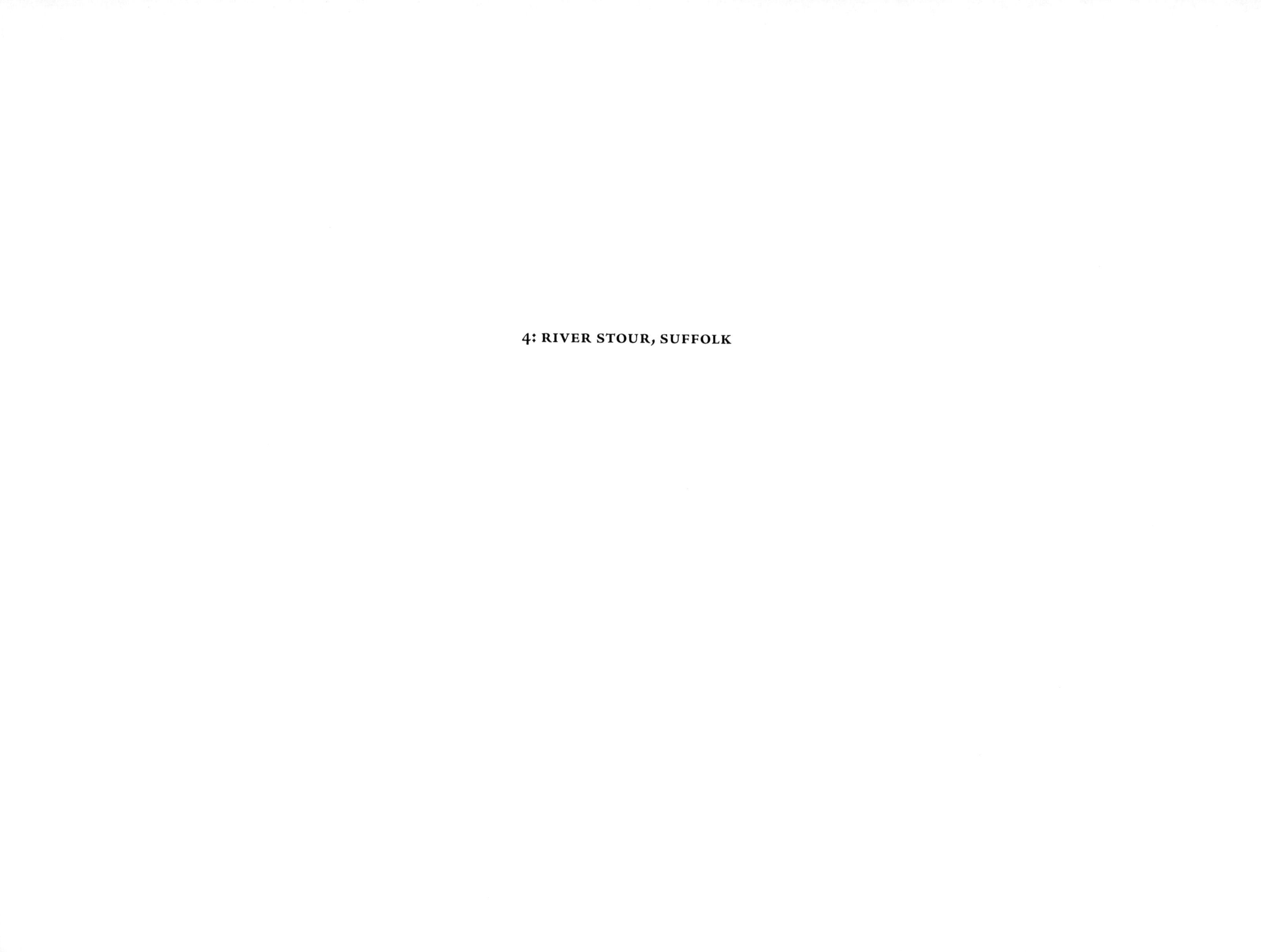

4: RIVER STOUR, SUFFOLK

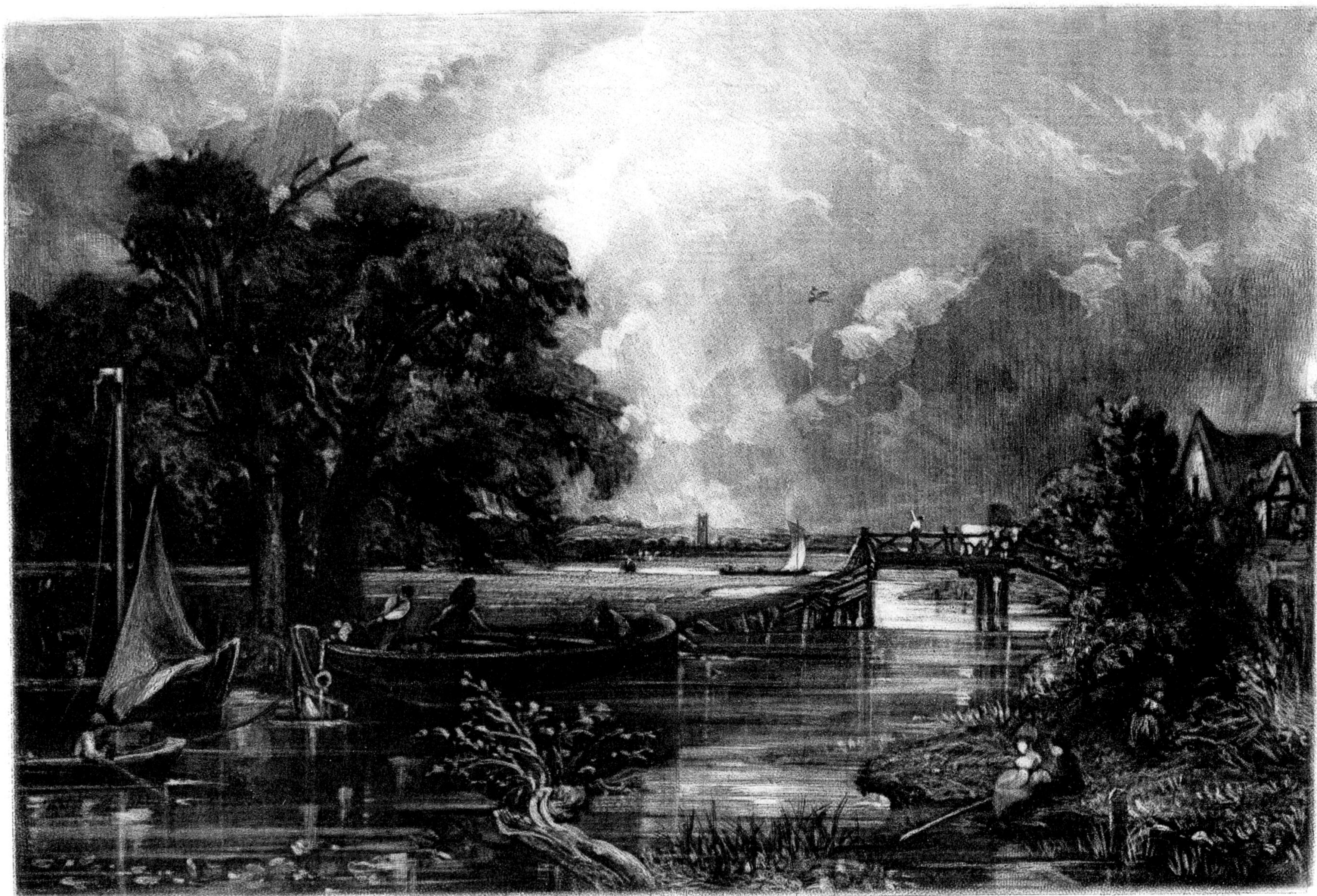

5: SUMMER MORNING

The Home Field, Dedham

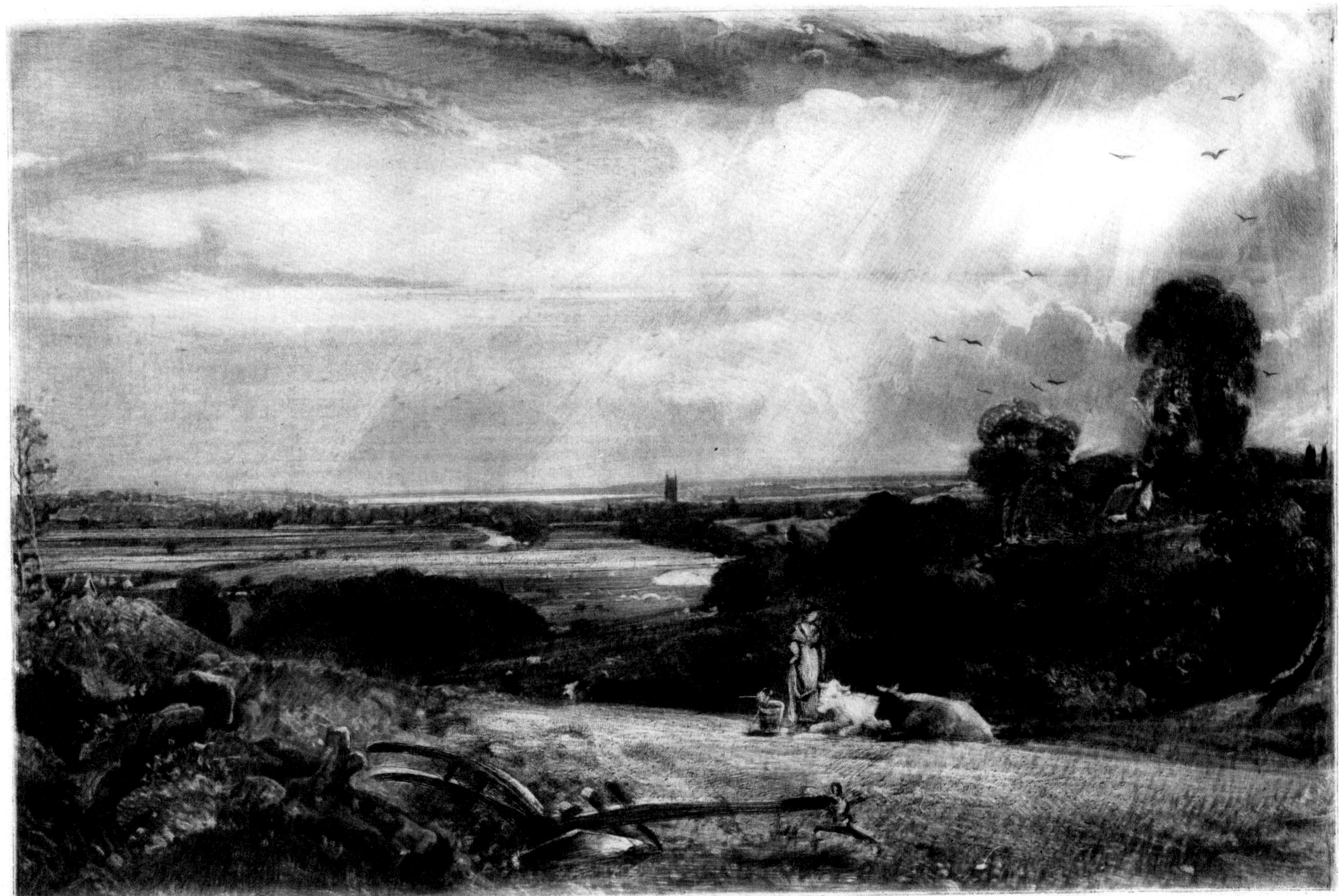

6: SUMMER EVENING

Cattle reposing, East Bergholt

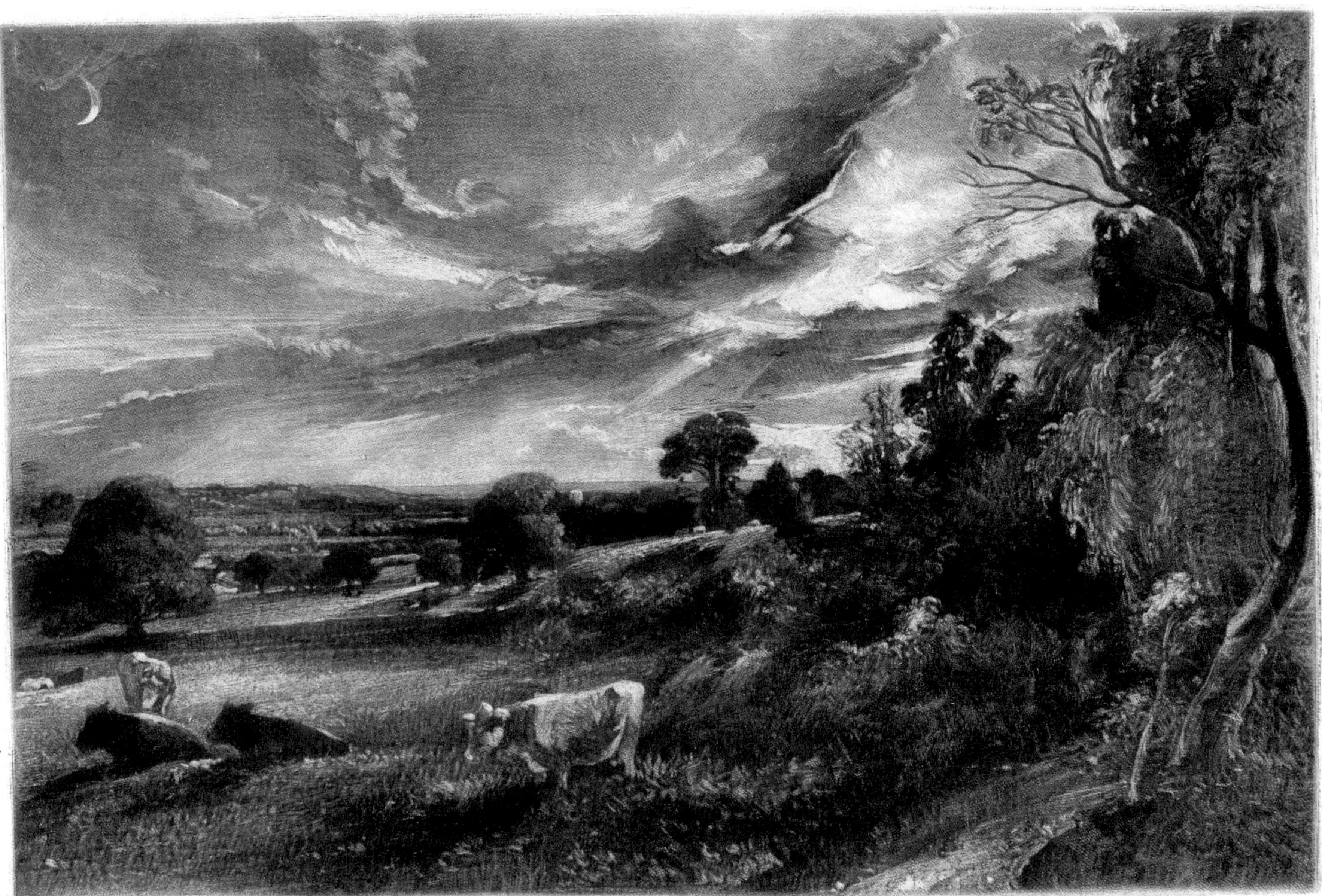

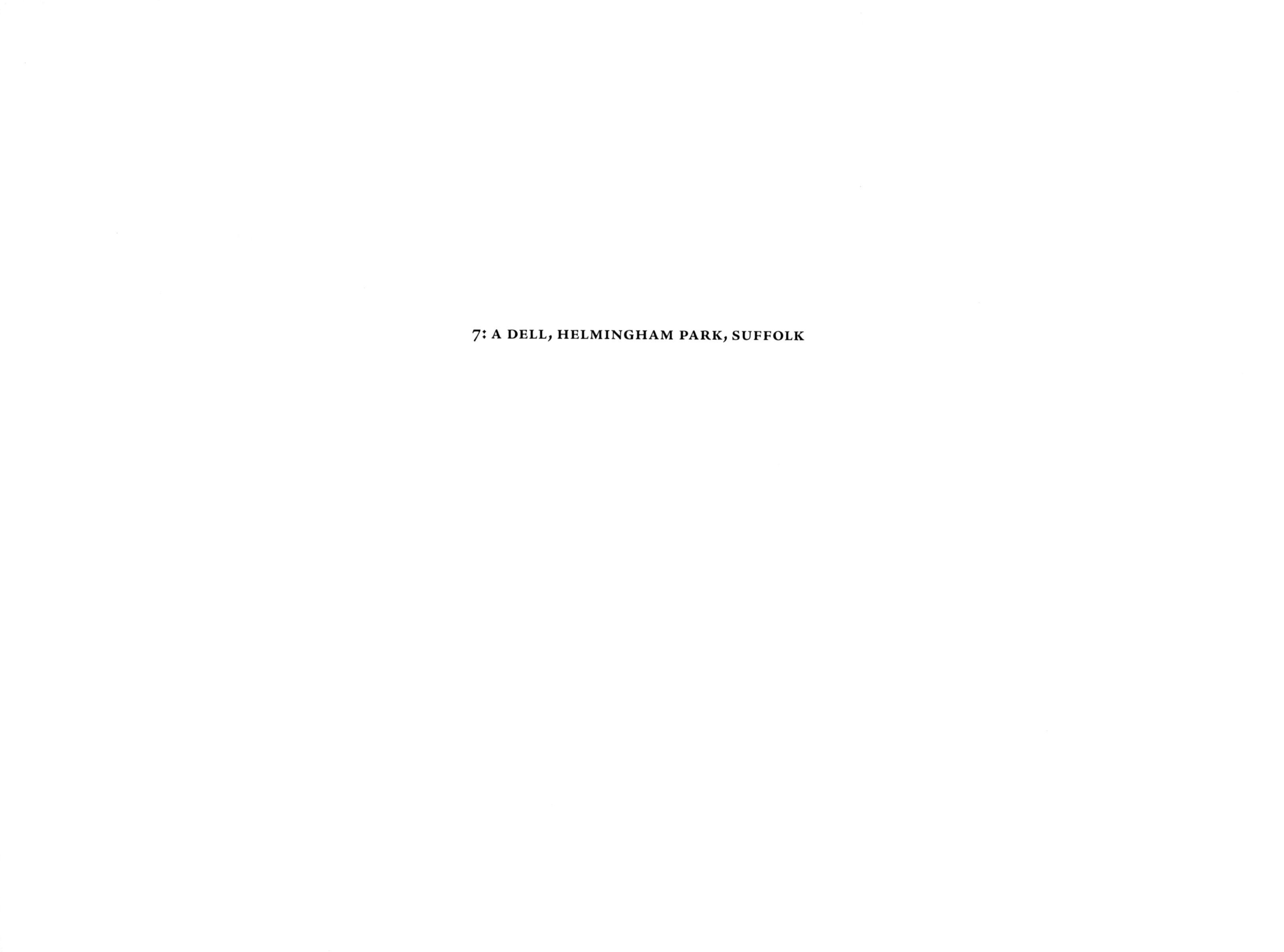

7: A DELL, HELMINGHAM PARK, SUFFOLK

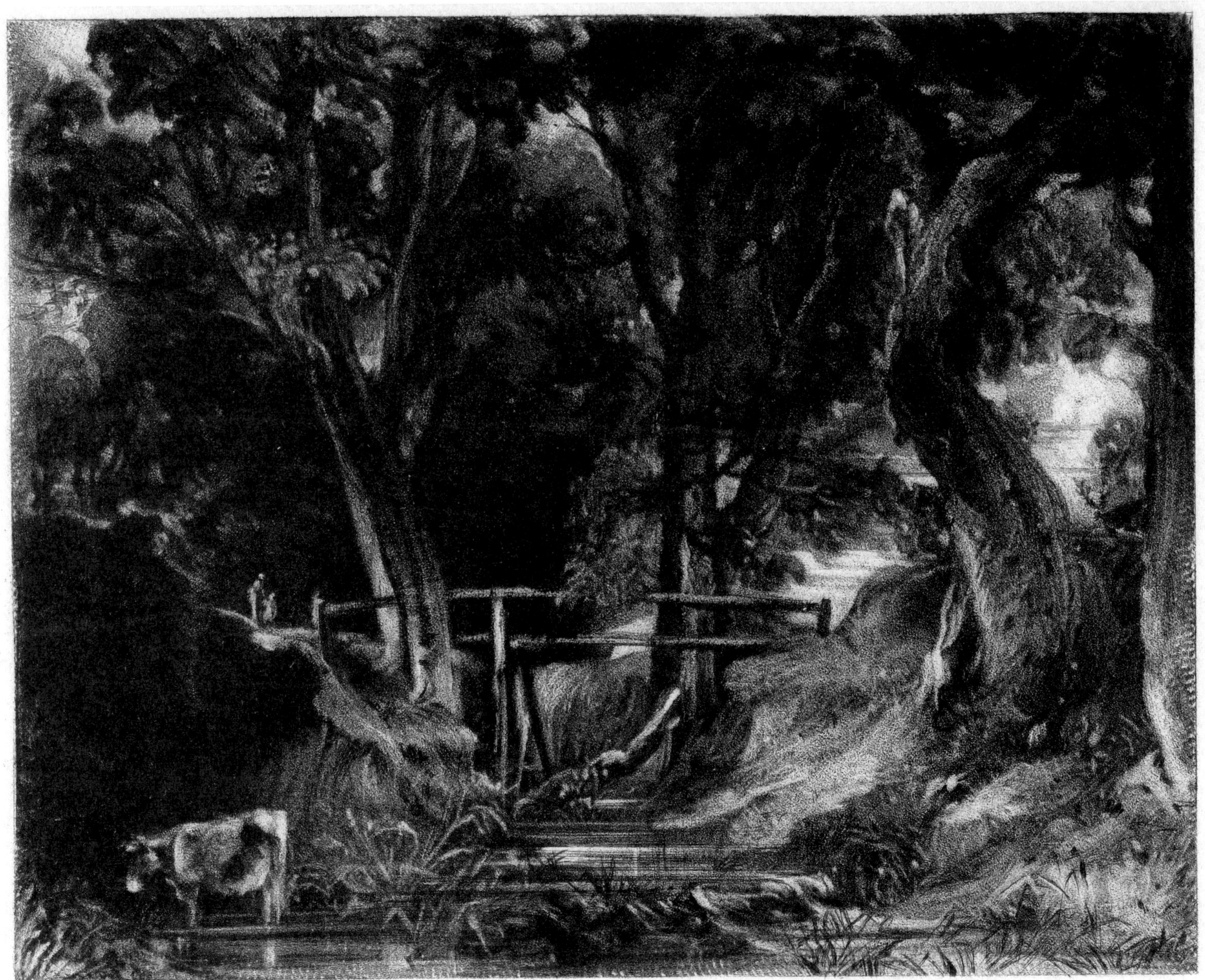

8: A HEATH

Hampstead Heath, Stormy Noon

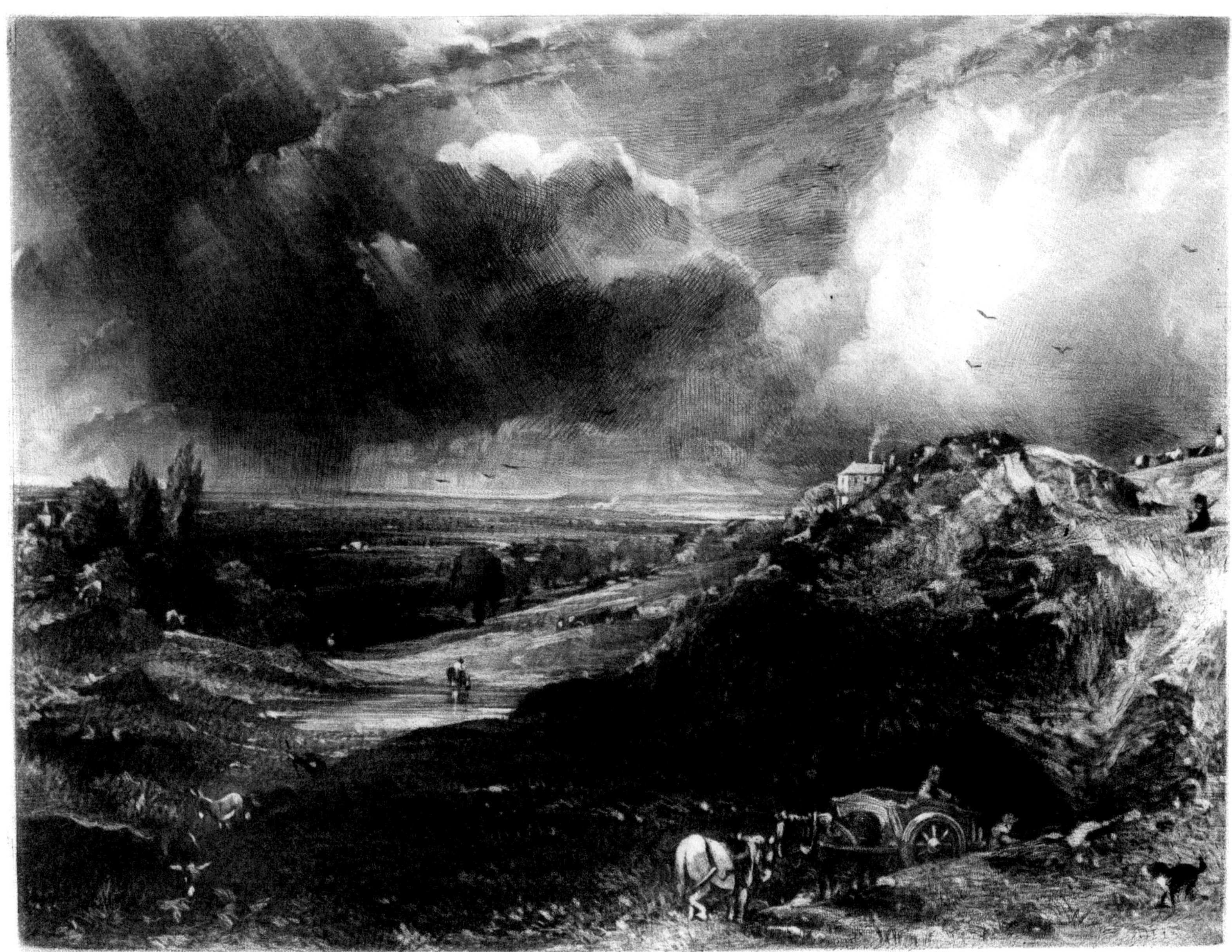

9: YARMOUTH, NORFOLK

Yarmouth Pier, morning

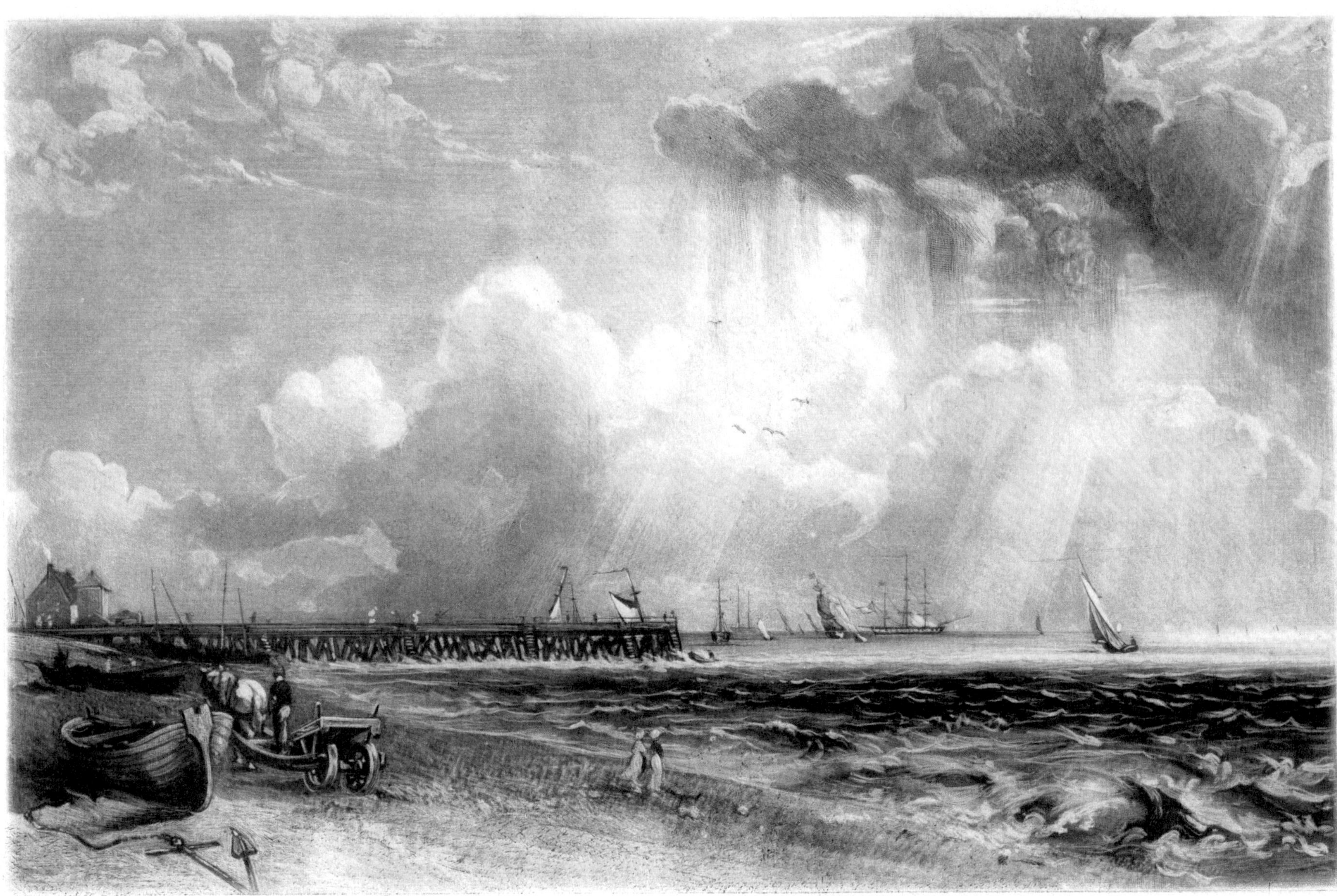

10: A SEABEACH, BRIGHTON

Brisk Wind

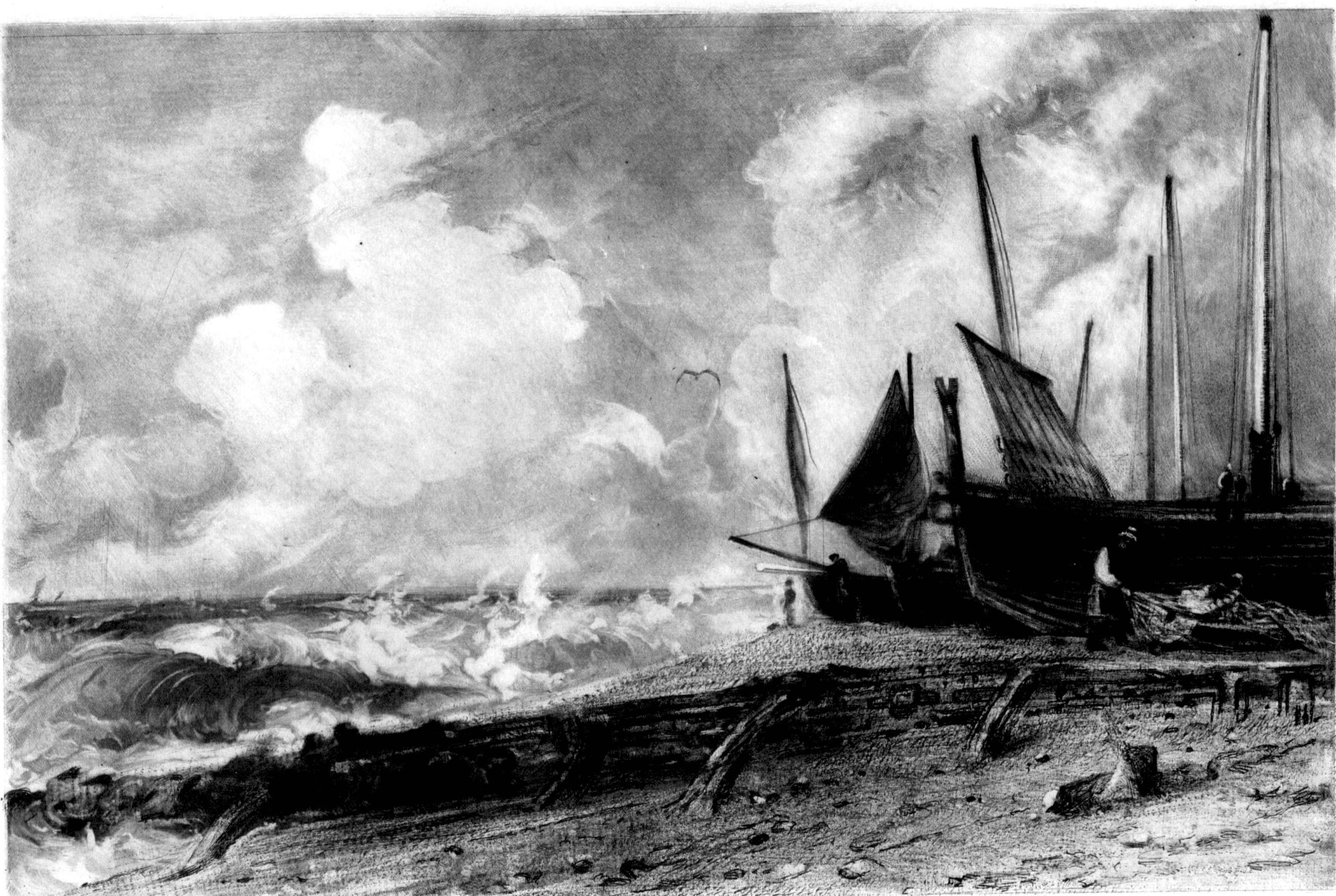

A SEA-BEACH, BRIGHTON

But nearer land you may the billows trace,
As if contending in their watery chase; [...]
Curl'd as they come they strike with furious force
And then re-flowing, take their grating course.*

The magnitude of a coming wave when viewed beneath the shelter of a groyne – and which is the subject of the present plate – is most imposing; as, from being close under it, it seems overwhelming in its approach – at the same time, from its transparency, becoming illumined by the freshest and most beautiful colours. The structures termed groynes, a kind of jetty, are numerous here; they are composed of timber in form and manner like a quay, but projecting into the seat at right angles with the shore. Groynes are admirable and indeed the only contrivances for preserving the beach and preventing the waves from reaching and undermining the cliffs: thus the shingle which on this coast is drifted from the west is arrested in its progress by them, and being so collected forms a beach which by its gradual slope and ample extent wards off the encroachments of the sea.

Of all the works of the Creation none is so imposing as the ocean; nor does nature anywhere present a scene that is more exhilarating than a sea-beach, or one so replete with interesting material to fill the canvas of the painter; the continual change and ever-varying aspect of its surface always suggesting the most impressive and agreeable sentiments, – whether like the poet he enjoys in solitude 'the wild music of the waves,'† or when more actively engaged he exercises his pencil amongst the busy haunts of fishermen, or in the bustle and animation of the port or harbour.

It is intended in this print to give one of those animated days when the masses of clouds, agitated and torn, are passing rapidly; the wind at the same time meeting with a certain set of the tide, causes the sea to rise and swell with great animation; when perhaps a larger wave, easily distinguished by its scroll-like crest, may be seen running along over the rest coming rapidly forward; on nearing the shore it curls over, then in the elegant form of an alcove suddenly falling upon the beach, it spreads itself and retires. In such weather the voice of a solitary sea-fowl is heard from time to time 'Mingling its note with those of wind and wave';§ when he may be observed beating his steady course for miles along the beach just above the breakers, and ready 'To drop for prey within the sweeping surge.‡ These birds, whether solitary or in flocks, add to the wildness and to the sentiment of melancholy always attendant on the ocean,

While to the storm they give their weak complaining cry.**

Of Brighton and its neighbourhood, now so well known, it is enough to say that there is perhaps no spot in Europe where so many

* George Crabbe, *The Borough*, (1730), lines 206-7 and 210-11.
† Untraced

§ Sir Walter Scott, *Letters on Demonology* (1830), p. 400. ‡ George Crabbe, *The Borough*, (1730), line 225
** Ibid, line 228.

circumstances conducive to health and enjoyment are to be found combined; and being situated as it is within so short a distance of the largest metropolis in the world, will account at once for its extraordinary rise, its vast extent and population, and the almost countless numbers who visit it during the season: also from having so long enjoyed the sunshine of a court, it has become an emporium of fashion, under whose shadowy auspices thousands still resort to it; and thus connected as it is with the metropolis, it has been aptly termed 'The marine side of London.'*

It is therefore no longer a matter of surprise that a change otherwise so incredible should have taken place; and that a fishing town of so little importance, should in the space of a few years have become one of the largest, most splendid, and gayest places in the kingdom; the resort of multitudes of every class of society. To hint at some of the natural local causes which have secretly wrought this change, and of which the thousands who are annually benefited by them are so little aware, cannot be irrelevant here. The situation itself – the most favourable on the coast – is between two considerable rivers, the Adur and the Ouse, into which all the adjacent rivulets flow, rendering the inland country dry and healthful. The neighbouring hills keep off the severer winds, and leave it open to the more genial breezes of the west, which coming from the sea preserve an almost equal temperature. Nor is this the only advantage derived from the contiguity of the hills: their nature being calcareous, they absorb all superfluous moisture, producing at the same time springs of the very finest water, which flow spontaneously in many places. The beach, though rugged and unpleasant, has yet a healthful quality peculiar to itself, for where the stones end the chalk again appears, leaving a pure and wholesome shore.

Of the climate, its salubrious qualities, though latent, are abundantly proved by the productions of the vegetable kingdom; since here may be found the fig, the almond, and the myrtle perfecting their fruit in the open garden; and since the establishment of a society for the encouragement of horticulture, few places in the kingdom can vie with Brighton in the excellence and beauty of her fruits and flowers: 'the pink-eyed Pimpernel'† here gives a silent but unerring testimony in favour of the climate, by its petals changing to a blue colour, a circumstance occurring only in the most mild and genial climates; and the remark that it is 'a country without trees, and a sea without ships,'§ will have little weight with those who have seen the flourishing condition of the trees and shrubs in the park, and even in the centre of the town, which prove what would have been the case had the country been planted. The want of shipping, or rather of their near approach, is compensated for by an advantage more than equal to the loss, as the point of Worthing to the west which keeps them distant, also prevents that accumulation of decaying weed on the shore, which forms so great an annoyance on many other coasts. Thus it will be seen that in this happily situated spot the climate, the inland country and the coast are equally propitious.

* Untraced. † Dr. Edward Jenner (1750-1823), 'Signs of Rain', line 10. Published in the *Gentleman's Magazine*, 1826

§ Untraced.

II: MILL STREAM

River Stour, near Flatford Mill

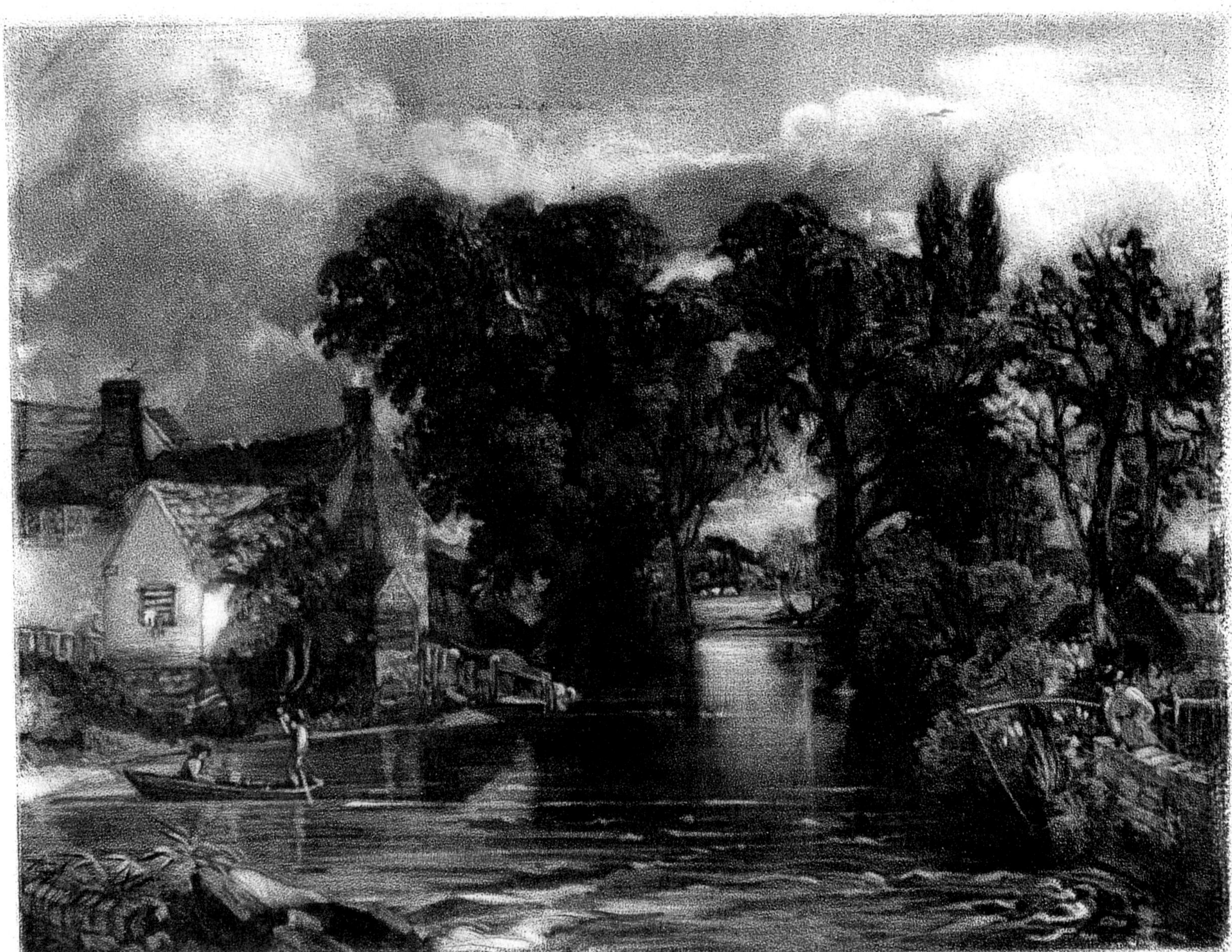

12: A LOCK ON THE STOUR, SUFFOLK

Head of a Lock, on the Stour

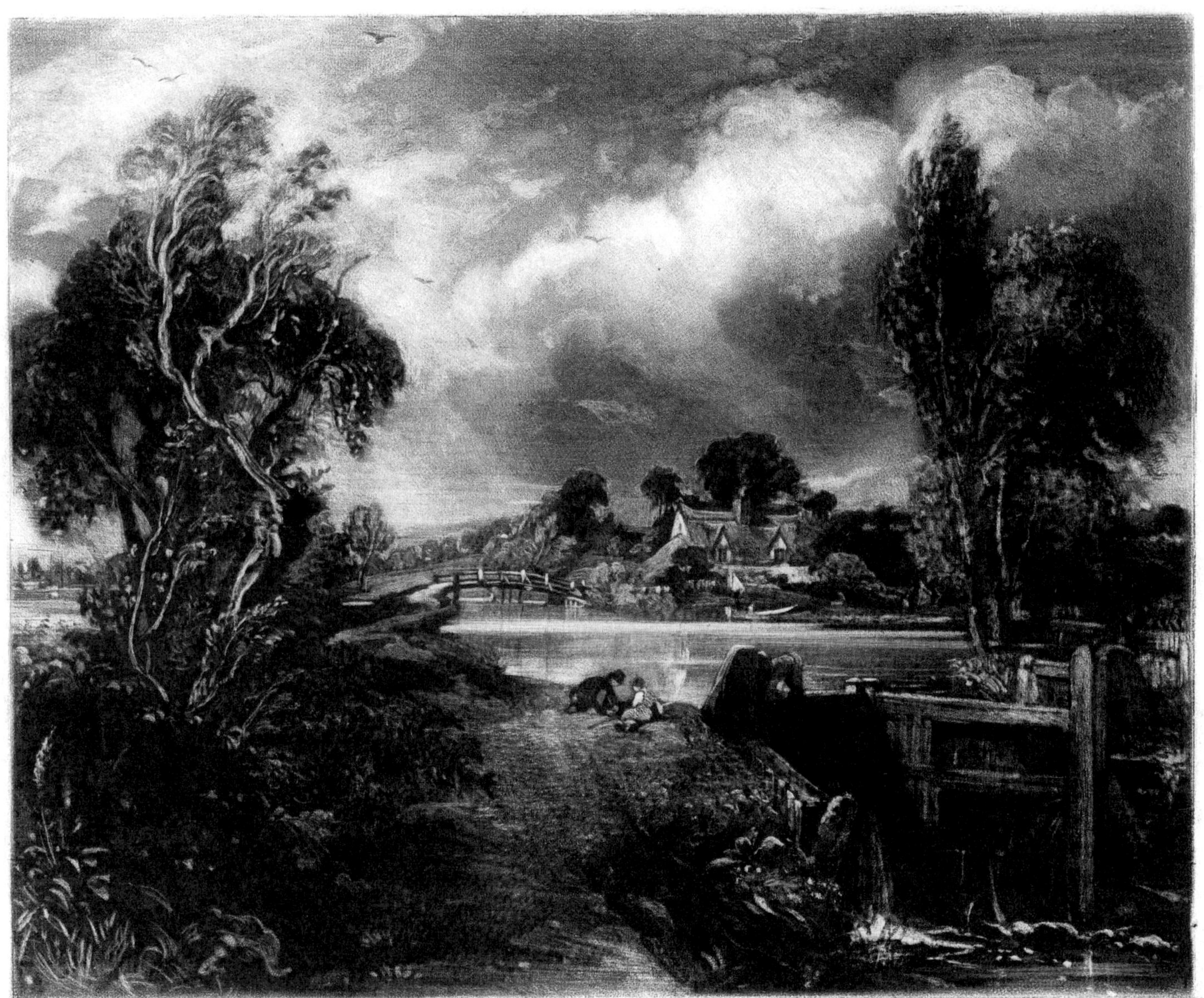

13: OLD SARUM

Mound of the City of Old Sarum

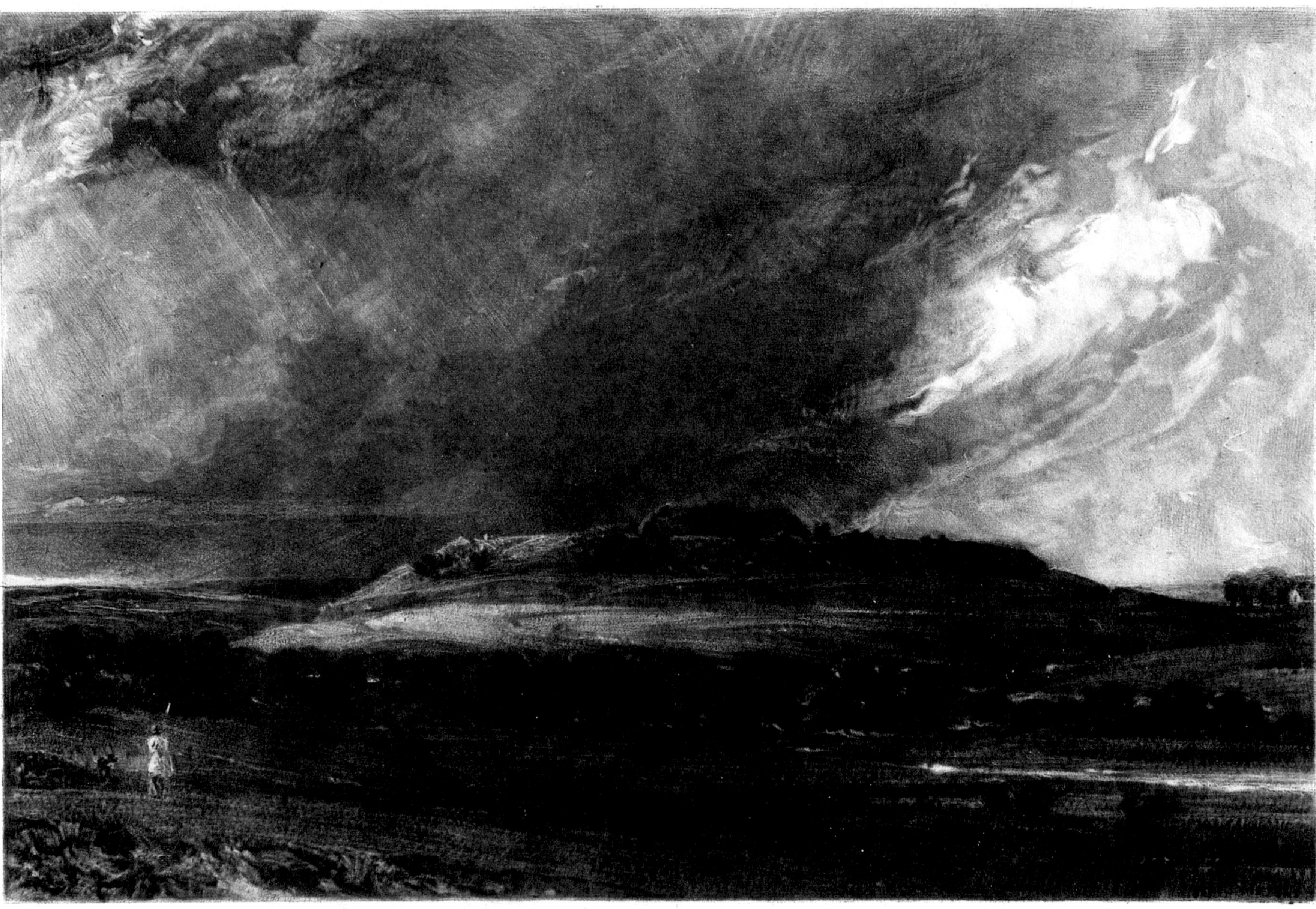

OLD SARUM

The pomp of Kings, is now the Shepherd's humble pride.*

In no department of painting is the want of its first attractive quality, 'General Effect,' so immediately felt, or its absence so much to be regretted, as in landscape; nor is there any class of painting, where the Artist may more confidently rely on the principles of 'Colour' and 'Chiaroscuro' for making his work efficient. Capable as this aid of 'Light and Shadow' is of varying the aspect of everything it touches, it is, from the nature of the subject, nowhere more required than in landscape; and happily there is no kind of subject in which the artist is less controlled in its application: he ought, indeed, to have these powerful organs of expression entirely at his command, that he may use them in every possible form, as well as that he may do so with the most perfect freedom; therefore, whether he wishes to make the subject of a joyous, solemn, or meditative character, by flinging over it the cheerful aspect which the sun bestows, by a proper disposition of shade, or by the appearances that beautify its rising or its setting, a true 'General Effect' should never be lost sight of by him throughout the production of his work, as the sentiment he intends to convey will be wholly influenced by it.

The subject of this plate, which from its barren and deserted character seems to embody the words of the poet – 'Paint me a desolation,'† – is grand in itself, and interesting in its associations, so that no kind of effect could be introduced too striking, or too impressive to portray it; and among the various appearances of the elements, we naturally look to the grander phenomena of nature, as according best with the character of such a scene. Sudden and abrupt appearances of light, thunder clouds, wild autumnal evenings, solemn and shadowy twilights, 'flinging half an image on the straining sight,' with variously tinted clouds, dark, cold, and gray, or ruddy and bright, with transitory gleams of light; even conflicts of the elements, to heighten, if possible, the sentiment which belongs to a subject so awful and impressive.

'*Non enim hic habemus stabilem civitatem.*'§ The present appearance of Old Sarum – wild, desolate, and dreary – contrasts strongly with its former greatness. This proud and 'towered city,'‡ once giving laws to the whole kingdom – for it was here our earliest parliaments on record were convened – can now be traced but by vast embankments and ditches, tracked only by sheep-walks: 'The plough has passed over it.'** It was on this spot the wily Conqueror, in 1086, confirmed that great political event, the establishment of the feudal system, which enjoined the allegiance of the nobles; other succeeding monarchs held their courts here, but during these periods, much must always be involved in that almost impenetrable gloom, which clouds the dark history of our

* Adapted from Oliver Goldsmith, *The Traveller*, (1730), line 36 (The pomp of kings, the shepherd's humbler pride.'). † Adapted from James Thomson, *The Seasons: Summer* (1730), line 113: [A faint erroneous ray]... Flings half an image on the straining eye'. § Hebrews 13:14. 'Stabilem' is a common substitution for the textual 'manentem'. ‡ John Milton, *L'Allegro*, (1645) line 117. ** Untraced.

Middle Ages; yet, doubtless, many were the ruthless acts of tyranny and deeds of violence perpetrated on this far-famed mount, but which have, alike with their agents, sunk into that repose of which its present appearance presents so striking an image. In the days of chivalry, it poured forth its Longspees and other valiant knights over Palestine. It was the seat of the ecclesiastical government, when the pious Osmond and the succeeding bishops diffused the blessings of religion over the western part of the kingdom; thus it became the resort of ecclesiastics and warriors, 'Of throngs of knights and barons bold,'* till their feuds, and mutual animosities, augmented by the insults of the soldiery, at length caused the separation of the clergy, and the transfer of the cathedral from within its walls, which took place in 1227, and this event was followed by the removal of the most respectable inhabitants. In less than half a century after the completion of the new church, the building of a bridge adjoining it over the river at Harnham diverted the great western road, and turned it from the old through the new city. This last step completed the desertion, and led to the final decay of Old Sarum. The site now only remains of this once proud and populous city, whose almost impregnable castle, and lofty and embattled walls, whose churches, and even every vestige of human habitation, have long since passed away.

The beautiful imagination of the poet Thomson, when he makes a spot like this the haunt of a shepherd with his flock, happily contrasts the playfulness of peaceful innocence with the horrors of war and bloodshed, of which it was so often the scene:-

Lead me to the mountain's brow,
Where sits the shepherd on the grassy turf
Inhaling healthful the descending sun.
Around him feeds his many-bleating flock,
Of various cadence; and his sportive lambs,
This way and that convolv'd, in friskful glee,
Their frolics play. And now the sprightly race
Invites them forth; when swift the signal giv'n
They start away, AND SWEEP THE MASSY MOUND
THAT RUNS AROUND THE HILL, THE RAMPART ONCE
OF IRON WAR in ancient barbarous times,
When disunited BRITAIN ever bled.§

* John Milton, *L'Allegro*, (1645) line 119

§ James Thomson, *The Seasons: Spring* (1730), lines 179-190. Emphasis from 'and' to 'war' Constable's.

14: A SUMMERLAND

Rainy Day. The Ploughman

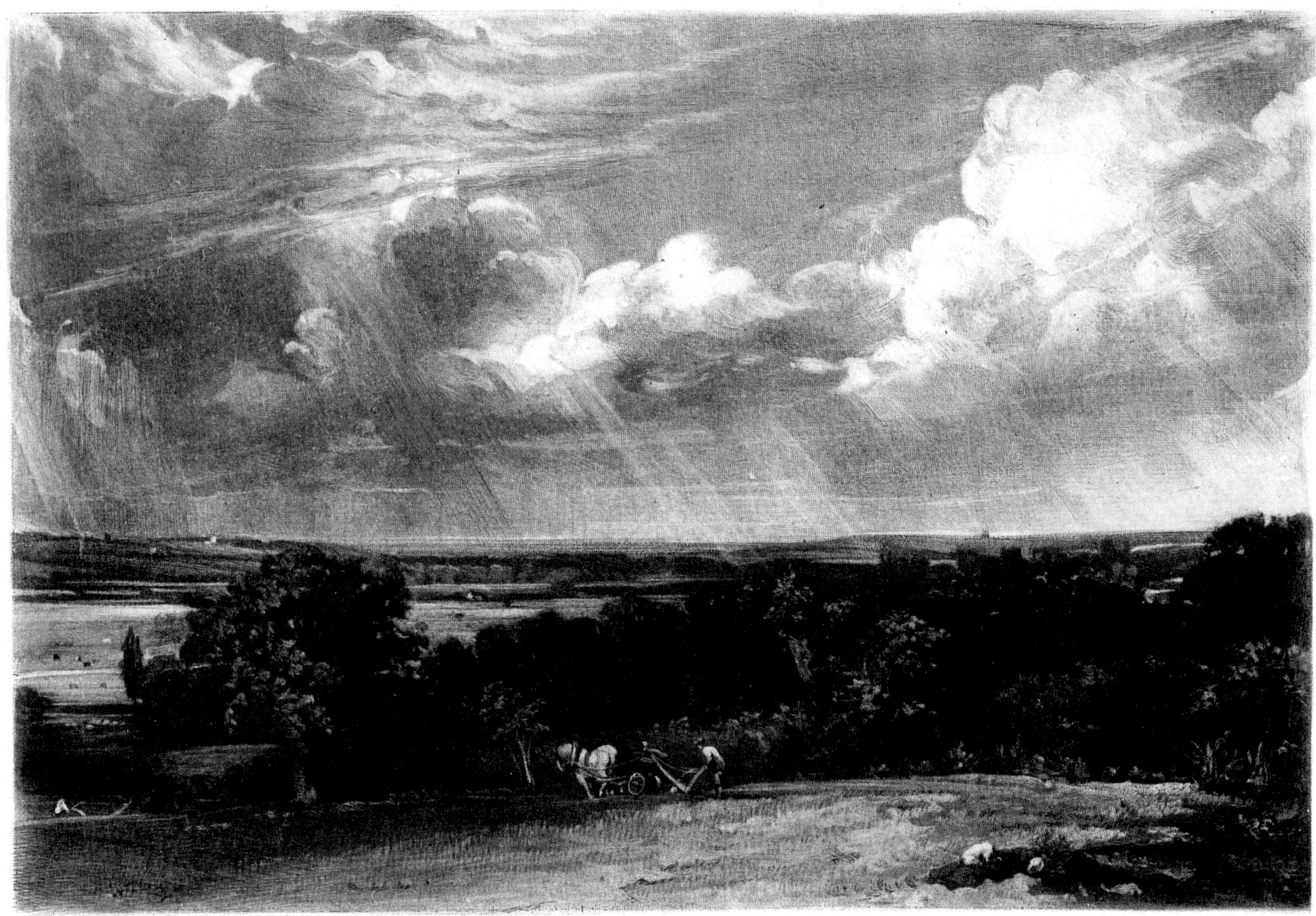

15: STOKE BY NEYLAND, SUFFOLK

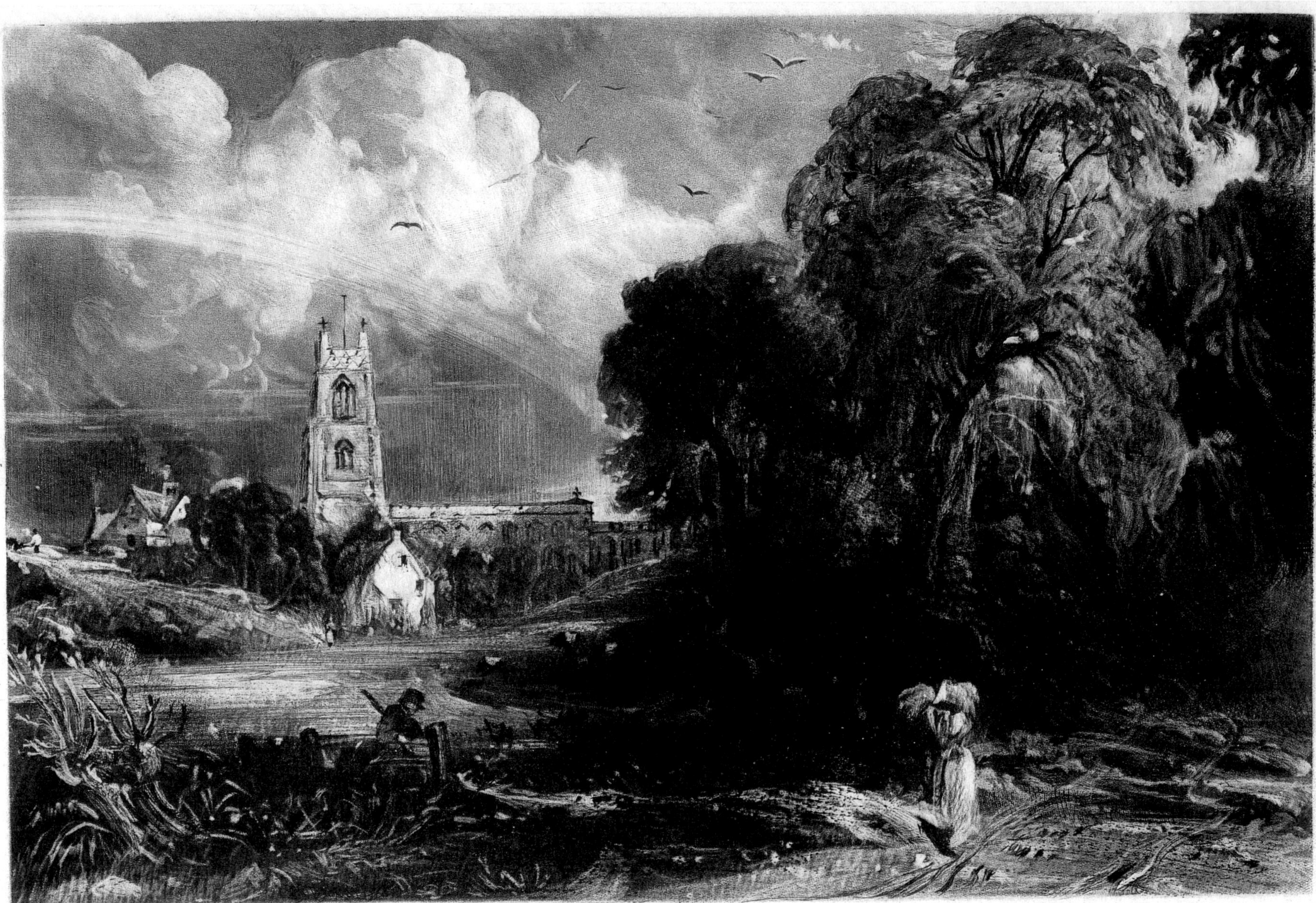

STOKE BY NEYLAND, SUFFOLK

Through the lighten'd air
A higher lustre and a clearer calm,
Diffusive, tremble.*

The solemn stillness of nature in a summer's noon, when attended by thunder-clouds, is the sentiment attempted in this print; at the same time an endeavour has been made to give an additional interest to this landscape by the introduction of the rainbow, and other attending circumstances that might occur at such an hour. The effect of light and shadow on the sky and landscape are such as would be observed when looking to the northward at noon; that time of day being decidedly marked by the direction of the shadows and the sun shining full on the south side of the church.

Of the rainbow – the following observations can hardly fail to be useful to the landscape painter. When the rainbow appears at noon, the height of the sun at that hour of the day causes but a small segment of the circle to be seen, and this gives the bow its low or flat appearance: the noonday bow is therefore best seen 'Smiling in a Winter's day,'† as in the summer, after the sun has passed a certain altitude, a rainbow cannot appear: it must be observed that a rainbow can never appear foreshortened, or be seen obliquely, as it must be parallel with the plane of the picture, though a part of it only may be introduced; nor can a rainbow be seen through any intervening cloud, however small or thin, as the reflected rays are dispersed by it, and are thus prevented from reaching the eye; consequently the bow is imperfect in that part. Nature, in all the varied aspects of her beauty, exhibits no feature more lovely nor any that awaken a more soothing reflection than the rainbow, 'Mild arch of promise';§ and when this phænomenon appears under unusual circumstances it excites a more lively interest. This is the case with the noon-tide bow, but more especially with that most beautiful and rare occurrence, the lunar bow. The morning and evening bows are more frequent than those at noon, and are far more imposing and attractive from their loftiness and span; the colours are also more brilliant, 'Flashing brief splendour through the clouds awhile.'‡ For the same reason the exterior or secondary bow is at these times also brighter, but the colours of it are reversed. A third, and even fourth bow, may sometimes be seen, with the colours alternating in each; these are always necessarily fainter, from the quantity of light lost at each reflection within the drop, according to the received principles of the bow. Perhaps more remains yet to be discovered as to the cause of this most beautiful phenomenon of light, recent experiments having proved that the primitive colours are further refrangible. Though not generally

* James Thomson, *The Four Seasons: Summer*, (1730), lines 950–52. † Attributed to Francis Quarles (1592–1644), 'On Time', line 10.

§ Robert Southey, Sonnet 5 (sometimes 7) – To the Evening Rainbow' (between 1794 and 1799), line 1
‡ Ibid, line 6

observed, the space within the bow is always lighter than the outer portion of the cloud on which it is seen. This circumstance has not escaped the notice of the poet, who with that intuitive feeling which has so often anticipated the discoveries of the philosopher, remarks:

> And all within the arch appeared to be
> Brighter than that without.*

Suffolk, and so many of the eastern counties, abound in noble Gothic churches: the size of many of them, and seen as they now are standing in solitary and imposing grandeur in neglected and almost deserted spots, imparts a peculiar sentiment, and gives a solemn air to even the country itself, and they cannot fail to impress the mind of the stranger with the mingled emotions of melancholy and admiration. These magnificent structures are often found in scattered villages and sequestered places, out of the high roads, surrounded by a few poor dwellings, the remains only of former opulence and comfort; but ill according with such large and beautiful specimens of architecture. These spots were once the seats of the clothing manufactories, so long established in these counties, and which were so flourishing during the reigns of Henry VII and VIII being greatly increased by the continual arrival of the Flemings, bringing with them the bay trade, who found here a refuge from the cruel persecutions of their own country, enjoying many privileges in return for their skill and industry; and also afterwards, when by a wise policy still greater encouragement was held out to them by Elizabeth, whom the course of events had raised to be the glory and support of Protestant Europe. The venerable grandeur of these religious edifices, with the charm that the mellowing hand of time hath cast over them, gives them an aspect of extreme solemnity and pathos; and they stand lasting and impressive monuments of the power and munificence of our ecclesiastical government. The church of Stoke, though by no means one of the largest, must be classed with these: it was probably erected about the fifteenth century; and there is reason to suppose that the same architect also built the two neighbouring churches, Lavenham and Dedham. The nave of Stoke church, with its long continued line of embattled parapet, the finely proportioned chancel, with the bold projection of the buttresses throughout the building, would be the admiration of the student ,while its grandest feature, the tower, from its commanding height, seems to impress on the surrounding country its own sacred dignity of character.

In this church are many interesting monuments, giving their frail memorial of departed worth and power: amongst them are several of the noble family of the Howards; one in particular, in the south part between the high altar and the choir, where is interred, 'The Right Honourable Woman and Ladye, Catherine, some time Wife unto Iohn Duke of Norfolke,' who fell at the Battle of Bosworth Field. – She died A.D. 1452. Also one to Margaret, second wife of the same Duke. Here, as well as at Neyland, are many tombstones of the clothiers; being mostly laid on the pavement they are much worn and defaced, but are known to belong to them by peculiar small brasses in the form of a shield still remaining, on which are engraved the figure used by the defunct as 'The mark' by which his own manufactures were known, and usually here applied as supplying the place of armorial bearings.

* Untraced

16: A MILL

An undershot-mill, Dedham, Essex

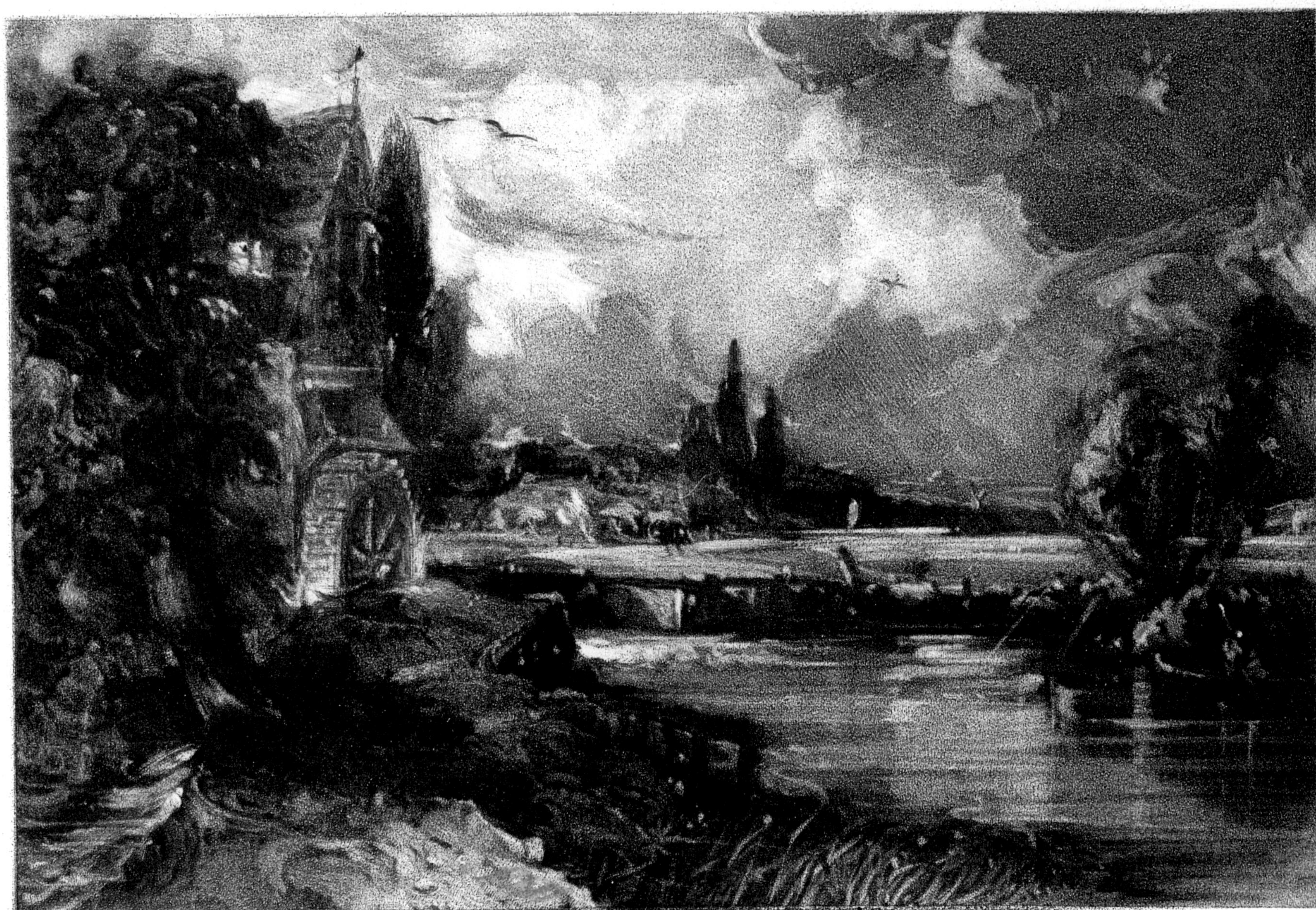

17: WEYMOUTH BAY, DORSETSHIRE

Tempestuous Evening

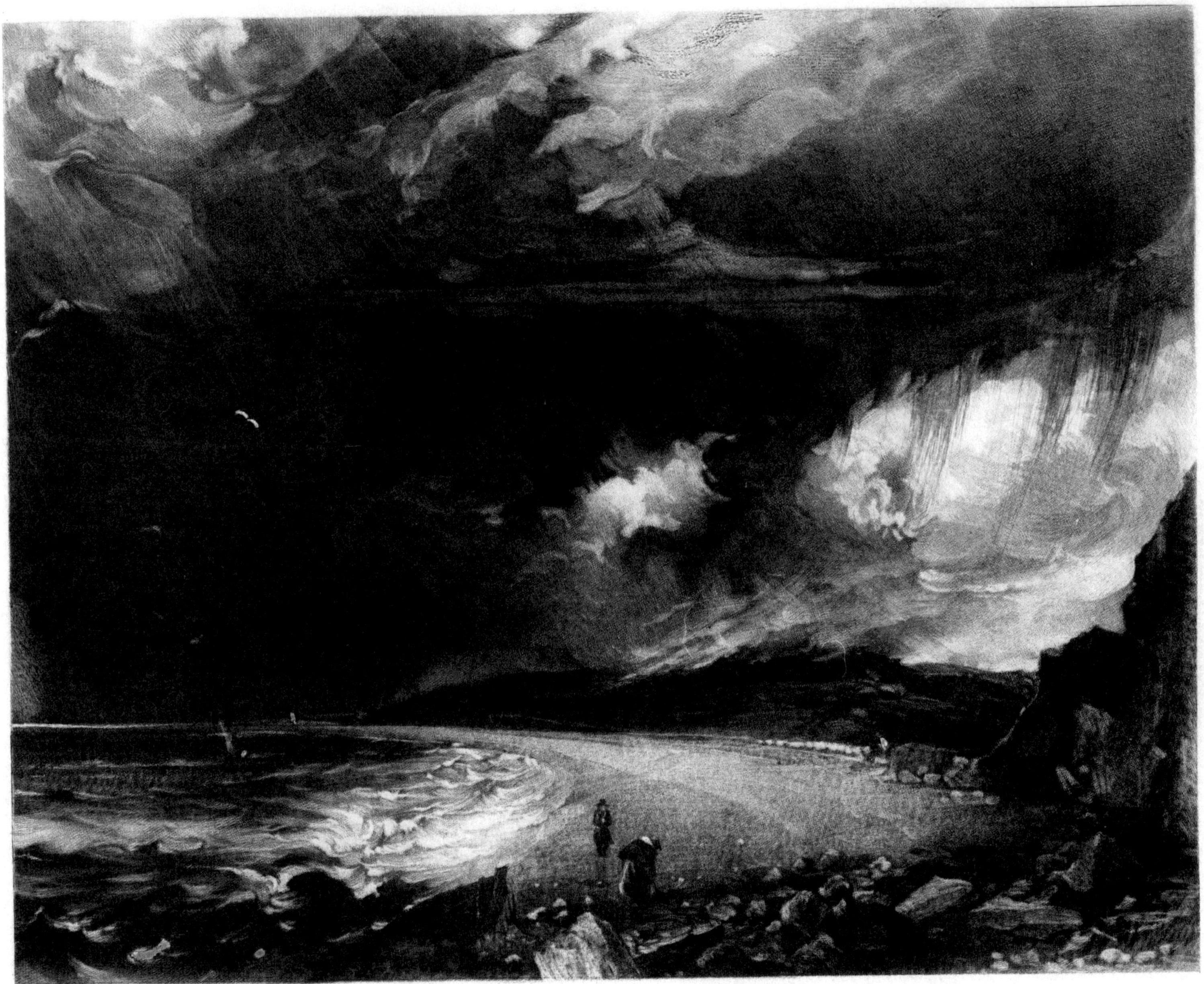

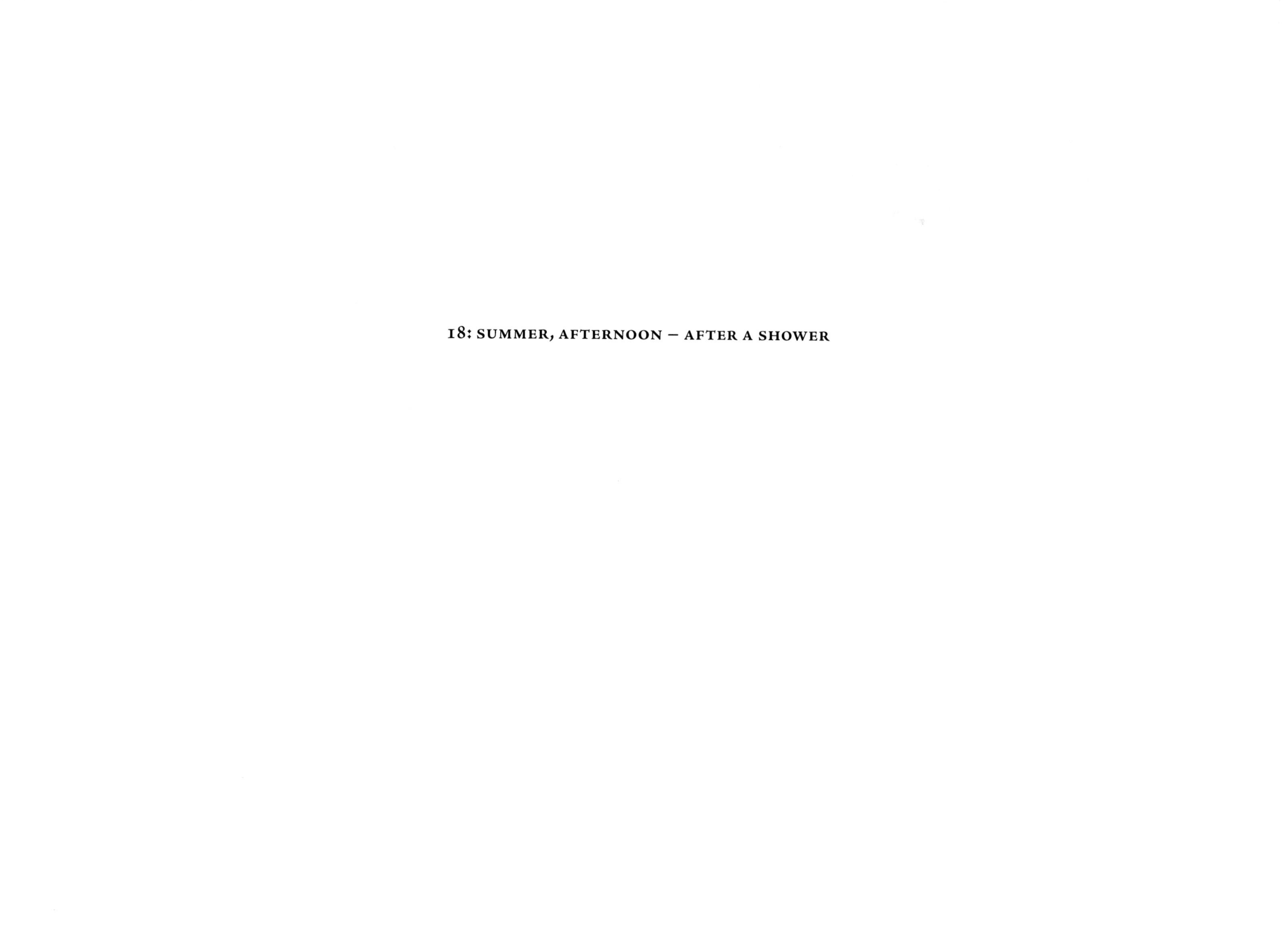

18: SUMMER, AFTERNOON – AFTER A SHOWER

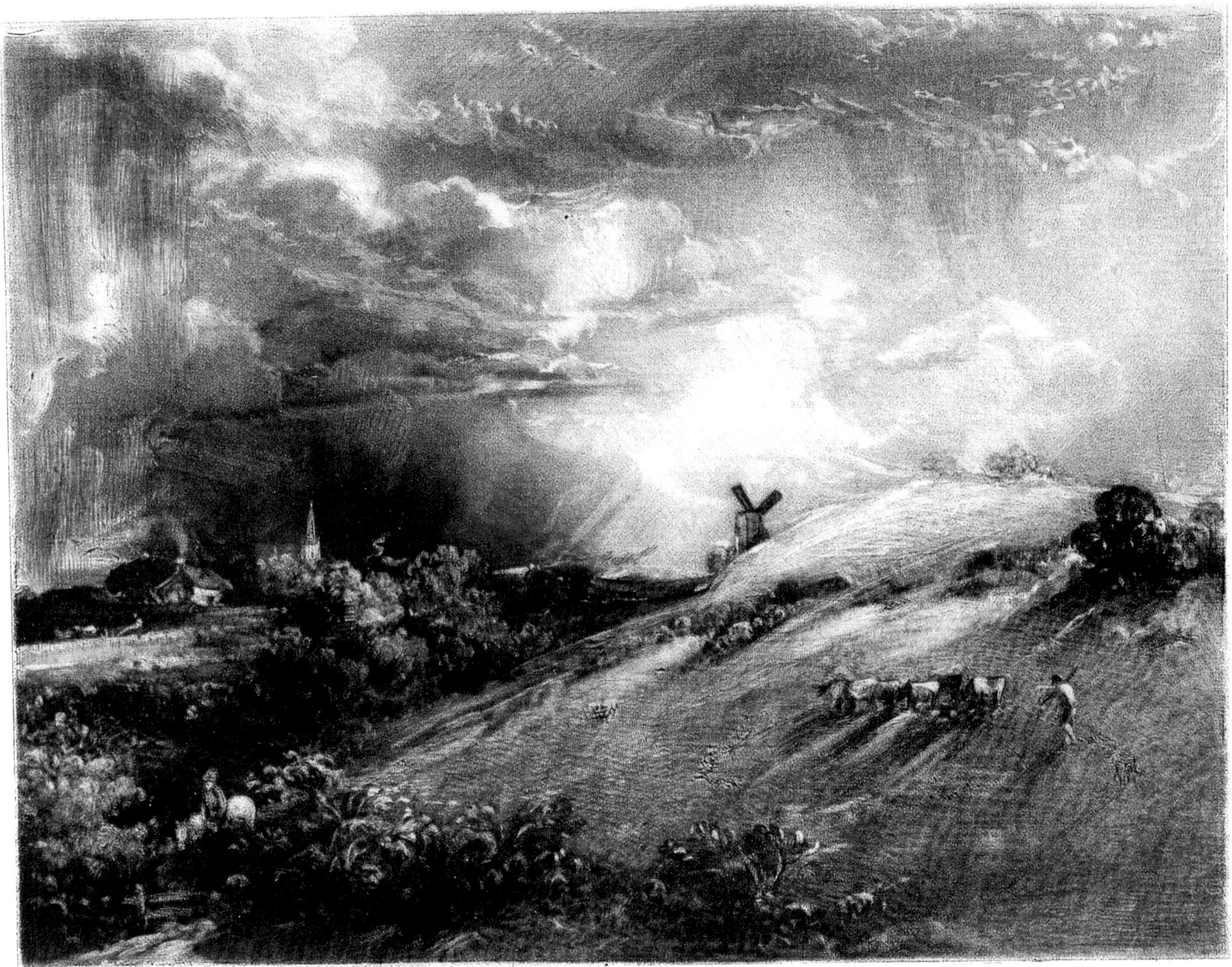

19: THE GLEBE FARM

The Glebe Farm and Green Lane. Girl at the Spring

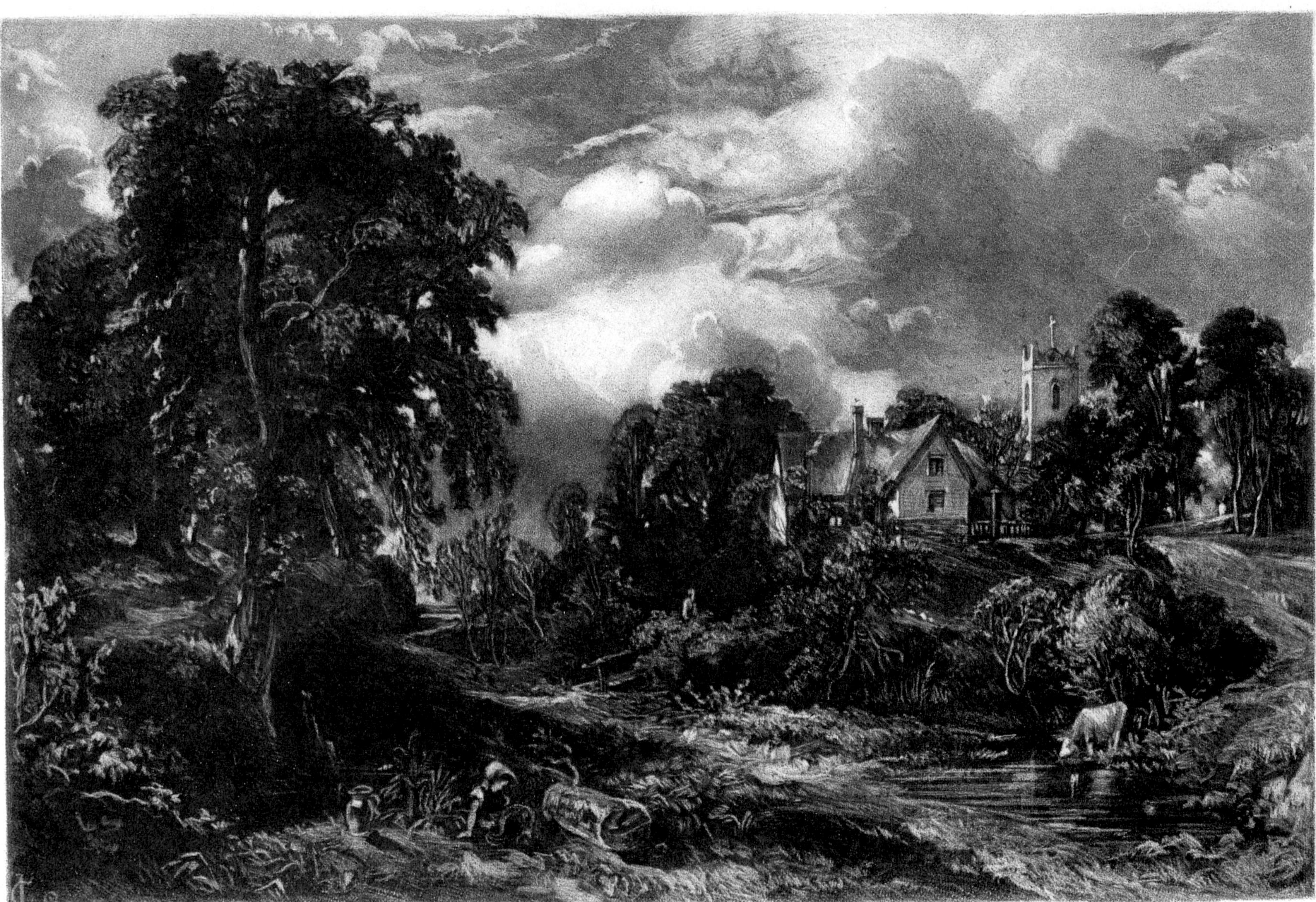

20: HADLEIGH CASTLE NEAR THE NORE

The Nore, Hadleigh Castle. Mouth of the Thames

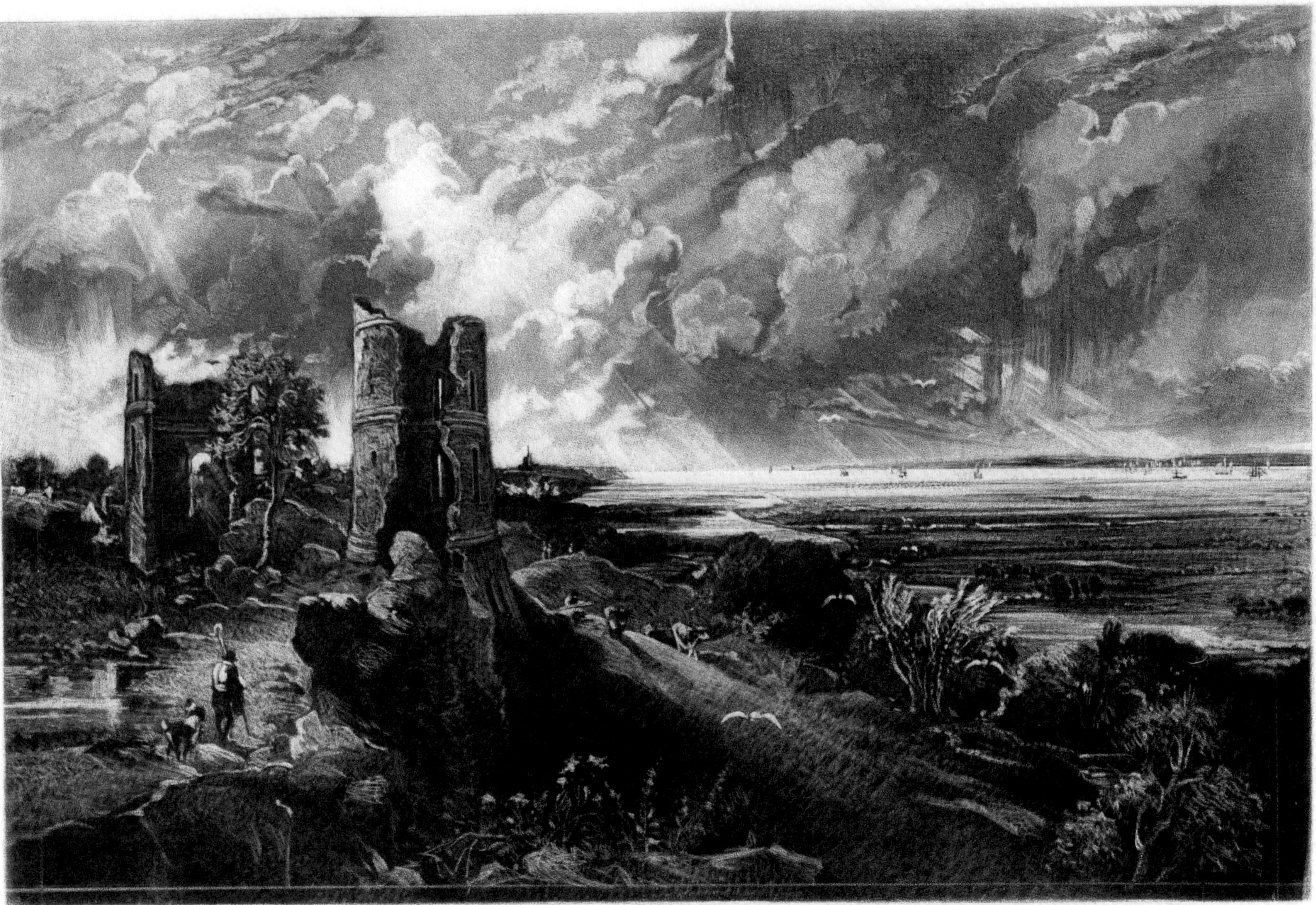

21: HAMPSTEAD HEATH, MIDDLESEX

The Latin tag, 'Ut umbra sic vita', 'Life is a shadow', was the motto on the sundial above the porch of St Mary's, East Bergholt

VIGNETTE.

To Mr. Constable's English Landscape.

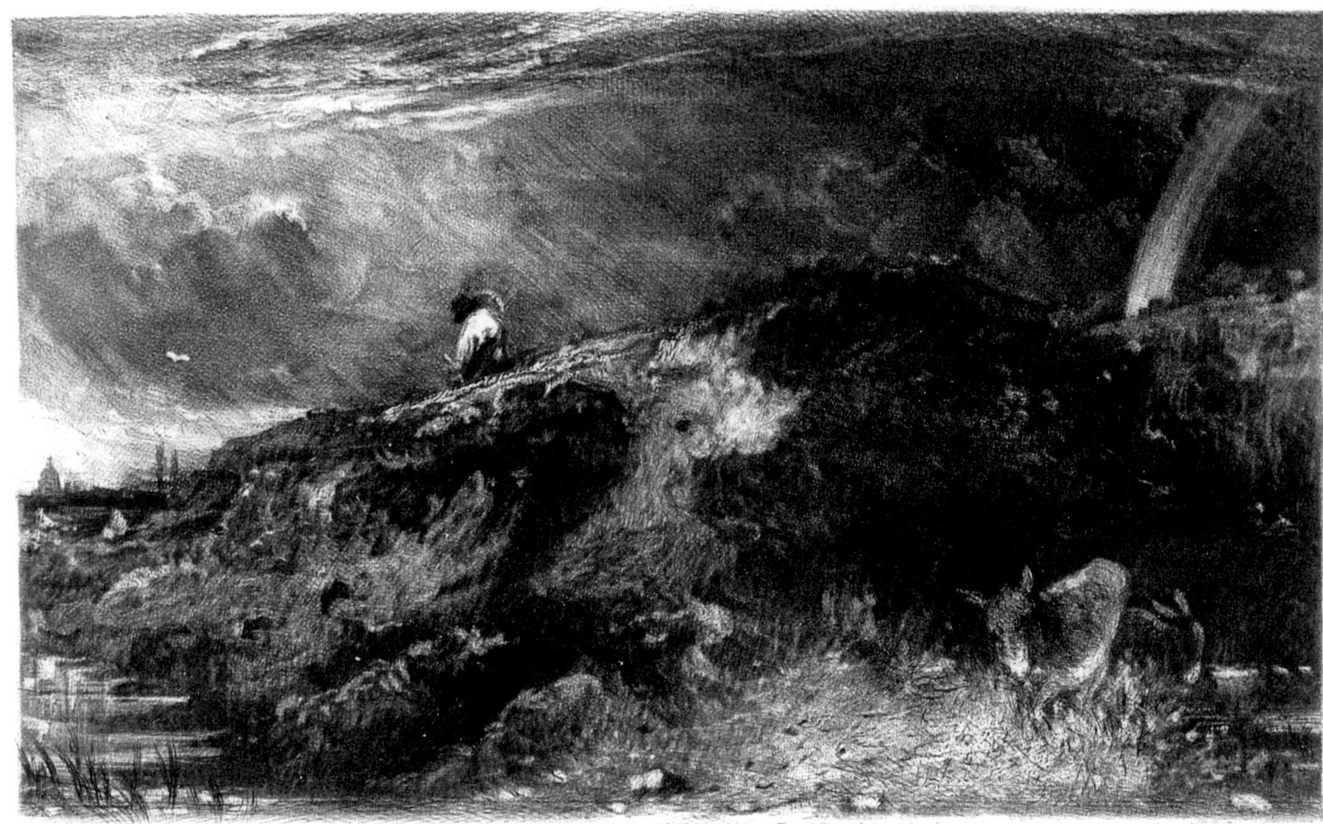

Painted by John Constable, R.A. Engraved by David Lucas.

HAMPSTEAD HEATH, MIDDLESEX.

"Ut Umbra sic Vita."

London, Published by John Constable, 35, Charlotte St. Fitzroy Square, 1831.